# THE SUBWAY SERIES

# THE SUBWAY SERIES

## BASEBALL'S BIG APPLE BATTLES AND THE YANKEES-METS 2000 WORLD SERIES CLASSIC

JERRY BEACH

SPORTS PUBLISHING

Sports Publishing books may be purchased in bulk at special discounts for sales promotion, corporate gifts, fund-raising, or educational purposes. Special editions can also be created to specifications. For details, contact the Special Sales Department, Sports Publishing, 307 West 36th Street, 11th Floor, New York, NY 10018 or sportspubbooks@skyhorsepublishing.com.

Sports Publishing® is a registered trademark of Skyhorse Publishing, Inc.®, a Delaware corporation.

Visit our website at www.sportspubbooks.com.

10 9 8 7 6 5 4 3 2 1

Library of Congress Cataloging-in-Publication Data is available on file.

Cover design by Tom Lau
Cover photo credit: Getty Images

ISBN: 978-1-68358-342-4
Ebook ISBN: 978-1-68358-343-1

Printed in the United States of America

To Helene Leavitt.
For being the best mother to my wife, mother-in-law to me, and grandmother to our daughter; and for the innumerable gifts and lessons Mom/Ma/Grammy provided us over her final 15 months.
We all miss you very much.

And to Molly.
A unanimous first-ballot Hall of Fame daughter and the light of our lives from the moment you arrived.

# CONTENTS

# ACKNOWLEDGMENTS

Officially, I was approached about writing this book in June 2019 and finished it just under five months later. But in reality, this project dates back to 1998, when I began freelancing for the Mets' official newspaper, *New York Mets Inside Pitch*, and in particular the wild, wild days of the first Internet boom—the fall of 1999 and the spring of 2000.

In fall '99, two of my college friends, Jeff Colchamiro and Dan Kline, started a lifestyle website, rouze.com, and hired me to write sports features. A few months later, Bryon Evje hired me to cover the Mets for the ACSSports.com family of websites, which, in the pre-MLB.com era, included the Mets' official website. Without those assignments, my career would have been much different, and I never would have built the relationships or the foundation to take on this project. *New York Mets Inside Pitch*, rouze.com, and ACSSports.com are long gone, but thanks to Coman Publishing, as well as to Dan, Jeff, Bryon, and my coworker at ACSSports.com, Steven Goldman.

During the 2000 playoffs, I met a mets.com intern, a college freshman whose impressive knowledge of Billy Idol's catalogue belied his age. Who could have imagined 19 years later that Bryan Hoch would not only be established as one of the nation's top beat writers at yankees.com, but that I would field a text from him (2000 me: "What's a text?") referring me to Sports Publishing's search for a Subway Series author? Thanks to Bryan for the two decades of friendship, which now spans three books.

Thank you to Julie Ganz, my editor at Sports Publishing, for entrusting me with this project on such short notice and for her guidance throughout the process. I hope things went as smoothly for you as they did for me. Thanks also to Jason Katzman for his editing assistance as we approached the finish line.

The inside photographs in this book come courtesy of Rob Cuni, whom I've known since he walked into the office of the small sports magazine I edited in the late 1990s and asked if we needed a photographer. We did, and I'm glad our friendship has lasted much longer than our time at that magazine. This is the second time Rob has contributed photos to a book I wrote, and I can think of no one else I'd rather have behind the camera.

None of this would be possible without a day job that had me at the ballpark on a regular basis. Thanks to my editors at Field Level Media, including Rick Kaplan and Jeff Reynolds, for all the opportunities there, and to my forbes.com editors, Brett Knight and Daniel Kleinman, for bringing me aboard as a contributor. Thank you also to Kolby Paxton, who asked me in June to contribute college basketball coverage to FloHoops.com and patiently waited until November—when college basketball had already begun—for me to begin writing for him.

I am appreciative to everyone who took the time to speak to me for this book. A full list of interviewees is in the bibliography, but I would like to extend extra thanks to Steve Phillips, Joe Torre, Bobby Valentine, and Todd Zeile for being particularly generous with their time. David Cone was also extremely kind and understanding when I told him I was late for our interview because we'd spent the morning putting down our 20-year-old cat (RIP, Maggie).

Thank you also to Brad Young of USA Baseball for setting up the interview with Scott Brosius. The public relations firm of Nicholas & Lence Communications—including Josh Knoller, Chrystine Nicholas, and Nick Nicholas—was extremely helpful in getting me some time with Mariano Rivera before the parade in his honor in New Rochelle, NY, in late July.

I didn't say much in the press box about this project, since I hadn't written a book in more than a decade and was petrified I wouldn't meet the deadline. So I offer the heartiest of thanks to Bryan Hoch and the other coworkers in whom I did confide: Laura Albanese, Billy Altman, Peter Botte (who also wrote a book last summer), Zach Braziller, Larry Fleisher, Howie Karpin, Bob Klapisch, and Scott Orgera. Their friendship, words of encouragement, suggestions throughout the process, and proofreading expertise were all invaluable.

Extra thanks to Bob, who shared with me some pivotal columns he wrote in the late '90s and 2000 for the *Bergen Record* and ESPN.com; and to Larry, who has the most impressive memory and research skills of anyone I know. I lost count of the number of times he'd suggest an angle or long-ago stat for the book and then have a link to a story from the 2000 season in G-chat by the time I got home.

Thanks to all the New York baseball writers who make the Big Apple such a great place to cover the best game in the world, and to the denizens of #MetsTwitter, whose passion makes that place so entertaining year-round.

I'd also like to acknowledge the Mets beat writers from 2000: Pete Caldera (*Bergen Record*), Rafael Hermoso (*New York Daily News*), Tyler Kepner (*New York Times*), Andrew Marchand (*New York Post*), Jose de Jesus Ortiz (*Newark Star-Ledger*), T. J. Quinn (*Bergen Record* and *New York Daily News*), Kit Stier (*Journal News*), and the late, great Marty Noble (*Newsday*). Their work was an invaluable resource then and now, and their kindness to a bespectacled kid from small-town

Connecticut trying to write on the Internet was and remains much appreciated. Thank you to T. J. as well as Bob Klapisch for writing the back cover blurbs.

I was a little more carefree with letting other friends outside the New York area know about the project. Thanks to my friends from my college basketball travels—Mike Brodsky, Dan Crain, Jaden Daly, Michael Litos, Gary Moore, Brian Mull, and Rob Russell—for their support and encouragement, as well as to Matt Pallister and Todd Stumpf.

Matt Edwards, my oldest and best friend from back home in Connecticut, was a constant source of support. So too were fellow Torringtonians Mark Arum, Emily Kline, Katina McGrath, Carrie Newton, and Mark Silano. Our off-color Facebook chats provided much-needed levity.

Thanks to my friend and accountant, Lloyd Carroll, for his advice, as well as to my unofficial lawyer (and official groomsman), John Guerriero, for his counsel.

I have been blessed with a family that's always encouraged me to pursue my passion for working in an uncertain and not-very-lucrative field, as well as for embracing—or at least tolerating—the quirks that come with it, including an unusual idea of a work day and a penchant for keeping a whole lot of stuff in case I might need it someday down the road.

In 2011, I helped my Dad, Jerry Sr., clean out the basement in his house, which he'd bought with my mother in 1990, when I was a high school junior. At one point, he realized most of the stuff in the basement was stuff I'd accumulated during my college years and beyond. He finally turned to me.

"Jer, have you heard of the show 'Hoarders'?

"Of course. Why?"

"Are—are you a hoarder?"

Sort of, but all those media guides and newspaper clippings in my basement made the research portion of this project much easier! Thanks for everything, Dad, and thanks to my sister, Eileen; her husband, Charlie; and my nephew, Matthew, for their constant love and support. Thank you as well to David Embrey, Matthew's Dad, and his wife, Tricia, for their friendship.

I must also thank my late mother, Maureen, for being the greatest person I'll ever know, and for continuing to serve as the guiding light of our family. Not a day goes by that I don't think of and miss you.

Thank you to Mom's family on Long Island, including my Aunt Gail and the Schoppman cousins. Despite all the aforementioned quirks of me and my chosen profession, my wife's family has always supported me and embraced me as one of their own—nobody as fiercely as my late mother-in-law, Helene, who is one of the people to whom I dedicated this book but who most assuredly deserves mentioning here, as well.

Thank you as well to my wife's grandmother (and our daughter's great-grandmother), Evelyn; my father-in-law, Robin, and his wife, Lynn; and my wife's aunt and uncle, Holly and Scott, and their daughters Allyson and Jenna. An extra thanks to the Besmanoff family—Harold and Marsha and their children, Dana and Brian—who watched Game 1 of the Subway Series with my future wife as well as her late grandparents and were the first people I told, 19 years later, that I'd just interviewed the family's favorite player, "Paulie."

Thank you to the parents of my daughter's closest friends—Karen Palermo, Amy Theuret, and Joseph Venezia—for their support and for the many times they babysat as I worked on the book.

It feels appropriate to write a book about the Subway Series, since baseball in New York served as matchmaker for me and my wife. I first met Michelle when she walked into the student newspaper office at Hofstra in the spring of 1994 wearing a 1961 Yankees jacket. I had a crush on her immediately, but it took until November for us to flirt with each other at a bar, where she asked if I'd like to go to Shea Stadium and wait for baseball season to start. This was after the World Series was cancelled following the players' strike, so there was a non-zero chance we'd be there forever.

It didn't take long thereafter to realize I wanted to be with her forever, and on June 29, 2002, we we got married and the Mets beat the

Yankees, 11–2. (Roger Cedeno stole home off Ted Lilly.) In between first toasts and first dances and the other revelry, we darted upstairs to catch as much of the game as we could on the TV in the bridal suite. I'm so fortunate to call her my wife, and to be emboldened by her belief in me.

A little more than 10 years later, we welcomed our beautiful daughter, Molly. Being her father is the greatest joy I'll ever experience, and I thank her for making me feel like the luckiest Daddy in the world every single day. Molly was very patient throughout the four-plus months during which I wrote this book—a span that included a long-planned trip to Disney World on which I must have been the only person toting books about Roger Clemens on the shuttles to and from parks—but once in a while she would give me That Look and ask, "You're STILL working on the book?" Not anymore, honey, and I look forward to paying back all the playtime I owe you.

Quotes I collected during one-on-one interviews for this project are generally denoted with a "says," with the exception of the Luis Sojo quotes, which were collected in a group interview prior to Old Timers Day in 2019. "Real time" quotes from the 2000 World Series and earlier are generally denoted with a "said" and credited to the source material if they were not spoken in group settings. There are four exceptions. The Billy Joel quotes in Chapter 1 were collected in a one-on-one interview in the Mets' dugout prior to Game One of the 2000 World Series. Several Mike Piazza quotes in Chapter 2 were collected during a one-on-one interview on July 9, 2000—the day after he was beaned by Roger Clemens—for a *Mets Magazine* feature. A handful of Steve Phillips quotes in Chapter 2 were collected during a phone interview prior to Piazza's Hall of Fame induction in July 2016 for a story I wrote for ViceSports.com. And several Phillips quotes in Chapter 3 were collected during a one-on-one interview in 1999 for a *New York Sportscene* magazine feature. All anecdotal information has been obtained from the books listed in the bibliography.

Any and all mistakes or omissions are mine and mine alone.

# INTRODUCTION

11:59 p.m.: October 27, 2000

New York City went 16,081 days between Subway Series, a span excused by the mathematics of Major League Baseball, if not the Big Apple's belief about its place in the baseball world.

Between the final out of the 1956 World Series and the first pitch of the 2000 Fall Classic, Major League Baseball expanded from 16 teams to 30. The World Series used to pit the top regular-season team in the American and National Leagues; but in 1969, the two circuits divided into two divisions, the winners of whom played each other in a League Championship Series. By 1994, there were three divisions and four playoff teams in each league, and any World Series team had to survive two rounds of playoffs before reaching the Fall Classic.

The most impactful and far-reaching moves were relocations, not additions. The Dodgers and Giants, who combined to reach the World Series out of the National League 23 times while representing New York and were part of 13 Subway Series against the Yankees, moved to California following the 1957 season.

National League fans in New York didn't have to wait long for a new franchise, but when the Mets debuted in 1962, they inherited only the colors of the Dodgers and Giants, not the success of their predecessors. The Mets finished a combined 343 games under .500 in their first seven seasons.

There were reminders of what used to be from 1962 through 1981, when the Yankees battled the Dodgers in the World Series four times and the Giants once. Later in the '80s, there were four regional World Series played elsewhere in the country, allowing the fans of the Philadelphia Phillies and Baltimore Orioles (in 1983), the Kansas City Royals and St. Louis Cardinals (1985), Oakland Athletics and Los Angeles Dodgers (1988), and the Athletics and San Francisco Giants (1989) to enjoy the ultimate battle for bragging rights.

The Yankees and Mets, meanwhile? They only finished in the top two in their respective divisions twice between 1969 and 1997. The closest New York got to a Subway Series reboot was in 1985, when the Yankees, sparked by Most Valuable Player Don Mattingly, and the Mets, led by Cy Young Award winner Dwight Gooden, both finished in second place with more than 95 wins. But in the pre-wild card era, all the teams, players, and millions of New York baseball fans got was a plaintive what-if.

A Subway Series seemed further away than ever before by the early 1990s, when the Yankees endured their longest World Series drought ever before embarking upon their first rebuilding project in generations and the Mets bottomed out with a 103-loss season in 1993.

But by 1996, the Yankees were World Series champions. They returned to the playoffs as a wild card team in 1997, when the Mets enjoyed a surprising 88-win season. New York came within a whisker of having both teams in the playoffs in 1998, when the Yankees won 114 regular-season games and the World Series and the Mets were eliminated from wild card contention in game no. 162.

In 1999, the Yankees and Mets finally reached the playoffs together, and a Subway Series nearly happened. The Mets fell two wins shy of winning the National League Championship Series and advancing to the World Series against the Yankees, who ended up beating the Atlanta Braves for their third title in four years.

Finally in 2000, the Big Apple got a chance to see its baseball teams battle for the biggest prize of all. The AL East-winning Yankees and NL wild card-winning Mets survived scares in the first two rounds to reach the World Series, with the locals winning their respective pennants at home on consecutive nights, October 16 and 17.

The Subway Series met expectations, with the teams matching each other over five tense and tightly packed games that dominated the city's attention and became national news in Game 2, when the simmering feud between Mike Piazza and Roger Clemens took a turn even the World Wrestling Federation couldn't have scripted as Clemens threw Piazza's broken bat at him.

Now, after 1,575 intense pitches spread out over six captivating days, the Subway Series might have been down to its final out. The Yankees were up, 4–2, and had their nearly-automatic closer, Mariano Rivera on the mound. But the Mets had the tying run at third base in Benny Agbayani and their most dangerous player, Piazza, standing at the plate.

Piazza took a called strike as the clock at Shea Stadium hit midnight. The Subway Series had hit a seventh day. A sellout crowd of 55,292, its loyalties divided, waited to unleash celebrations entirely different in tone and expectations. Would the Yankees cement their dynasty on enemy territory? Or would the Mets send the World Series back across the Triboro Bridge, to a Game 6 and another clash between Clemens and Piazza?

Rivera came to the set, reared back, and fired one of his patented cut fastballs. Piazza took one of his familiarly mighty swings, and connected, the sound of the ball hitting the sweet spot of the bat rising above the din of the crowd and the noise around Shea Stadium.

The ball flew toward center field, taking with it the anticipation built up over 54 years, and the real-time hopes and dreams of the players and coaches on the field, the fans in the stands, and the millions of viewers tuned in around the world. The Subway Series had been everything everyone could have wanted. Would there be more?

# CHAPTER 1
# GAME ONE

**Yankees 4, Mets 3 (12 innings)**
**Yankees lead series, one game to none**

**EVERY BASEBALL SEASON** in New York began with the daydream: What if the Yankees and Mets meet in the World Series? But never did the possibility seem as real as it did in the spring of 2000, when the Yankees were coming off a second straight championship and their third in four years while the Mets were looking to build on their deepest trip into the playoffs in more than a decade, a six-game loss to the Atlanta Braves in the 1999 National League Championship Series.

Alas, as the playoffs approached in 2000, it seemed as if the Subway Series drought would continue. The Mets were in control of the NL wild card race for most of the season, clinched a playoff berth on September 27, and finished eight games better than the wild card runner-up, the Los Angeles Dodgers.

Among the Mets' 94 regular-season victories was a stunning 11–8 win over the Braves on June 30 in which they scored 10 runs in the eighth inning, including eight with two outs. But the Mets could not parlay that into a long-awaited division title. The Mets led the NL East for one day—by a half-game on September 1—before the Braves pulled away and locked up their ninth straight NL East crown.

Counting the postseason, the Braves were 29–14 against the Mets since 1998, including 18–3 at home. How confident could the Mets feel if the road to a pennant went through Atlanta?

Speaking of confidence, the Yankees weren't eliciting much of it by the end of September, either. A team that appeared through much of the season to be cruising to another division title and on pace to once again approach 100 wins barely staggered to the finish line. The Yankees, who were 84–59 through September 13, lost 15 of their final 18 games—only the fifth time since World War II that the team lost at least 15 times in an 18-game span. They were outscored by a whopping 89 runs during the skid, the worst run differential of any major league team over an 18-game stretch in 2000.

The Yankees ended the season by losing their final seven games and backed into the AL East title on the final Friday of the season when the Boston Red Sox lost. Despite winning the division, the Yankees reached the postseason with the fewest victories (87) of any AL playoff team—four fewer than the wild card, the Seattle Mariners.

The extended losing streak infuriated owner George Steinbrenner, who reportedly took out his frustrations on the employees in the Yankees' Tampa offices and left Joe Torre digging deeper than ever into his bag of motivational tricks.

"We had so much pressure in September that I remember when we clinched in Baltimore—we were carrying the champagne with us—I had a meeting before the game," Torre says. "I said, 'What do you say we drink it before the game?' I was trying to just lighten the mood because every time we looked up, we were five runs down."

The tailspin meant the Yankees would join the Mets in opening the playoffs on the road out west—the Yankees against the Oakland Athletics and the Mets against the San Francisco Giants.

A Subway Series seemed even further away when both New York teams lost their Division Series openers. But the Mets dodged disaster in Game Two, when Armando Benitez gave up a game-tying homer to J.T. Snow in the ninth inning before Jay Payton delivered an RBI single in the 10th and John Franco struck out potential winning run Barry Bonds to close out a 5–4 win.

That victory sparked the Mets, who earned a 3–2 win in Game Three at Shea Stadium on Benny Agbayani's walk-off homer in the 13th inning. The dramatic victory capped a pivotal day for the Mets: hours earlier, the St. Louis Cardinals completed a three-game sweep of the Braves with a 7–1 win.

The Mets clinched their NLDS the next day in Game Four, when soft-tossing right-hander Bobby Jones, who had a 5.06 ERA in the regular season, threw the game of his life—a one-hitter in which the lone hit, a leadoff double by Jeff Kent in the fifth, barely eluded the outstretched glove of a leaping Robin Ventura—in a 4–0 victory.

The road out of the Division Series was more eventful for the Yankees. Andy Pettitte and Mariano Rivera combined on a six-hitter in a 4–0 Game Two win before the Yankees returned home and went ahead in the series with a 4–2 win in Game Three. But with a chance to finish off the Athletics and finally endear himself to Yankees fans in Game Four, Roger Clemens added another spotty line to his postseason résumé by giving up six runs in five innings as the Athletics cruised to an 11–1 win.

That forced a decisive Game Five in Oakland, which, thanks to a quirk in the postseason scheduling, would be played the very next day without the usual off-day for travel. By any measure, the quick turnaround was a bigger challenge for the Yankees, who were losers of 17 of their last 22 games and had 21 players age 30 or older. The Athletics were 24–9 since September 1 and had just 10 players 30 or older.

Unfortunately for the Athletics, 22-year-old third baseman Eric

Chavez managed to motivate the Yankees during batting practice, when his pregame press conference was aired on the Oakland Coliseum scoreboard. Most of his comments were innocuous enough, but in the playoffs, it doesn't take much for someone's words to serve as bulletin board material for the opponent.

Asked what he thought about the possibility the Athletics could end the Yankees' dynasty, Chavez grinned.

"I don't mind at all. I mean, they've won enough times. It's time for some other people to have some glory here. But no, they've had a great run. I mean, it's hard to stay no. 1. Everybody's gunning for you, everybody's trying to beat you. They're going to throw their best at you. They've done a phenomenal job as it is. But it's time. I think tonight, if we can get this game, I think people are going to start looking at this team for years to come as hopefully starting something that they accomplished a couple years ago and have done the last couple years."

In shallow center field, four Yankees watched intently.

"I'll never forget that day," Jose Vizcaino says. "We were shagging behind second base and we were just listening to Chavez talking and he says, 'Oh, tonight the Yankee dynasty's going to be over' and all that. Never forget that. I was shagging with Jeter, Tino, [and] Posada. They came up to me and said, 'See, we don't do that stuff. That's not us. We talk on the field.'"

Whether it was Chavez's words, or the flat offerings of Athletics starter Gil Heredia as catalyst, the Yankees scored six first-inning runs. The Athletics closed within 7–5 and chased Pettitte in the fourth, but Mike Stanton, normally part of the Yankees' late-inning bullpen machine, entered with the go-ahead run at the plate and induced Chavez to ground out to begin a stretch of 5 ⅓ scoreless innings by a quartet of Yankees relievers. Chavez was the potential tying run again in the ninth, when he popped up against Mariano Rivera for the final out.

The dynasty was still alive, and for the second straight season, both New York teams were a step away from the Subway Series. The paths to a long-awaited October clash, so filled with potholes just a week earlier, were far more wide-open for each club. While the Mets no longer had to worry about the Braves, the Yankees had home field advantage in the AL Championship Series because the wild card Mariners knocked off the AL Central champion Cleveland Indians.

And both teams enjoyed series wins that doubled as coronations and allowed fans of the Mets and Yankees—and the members of the Mets, if not necessarily the Yankees—to savor a countdown to a Subway Series more than four decades in the making.

The Mariners beat the Yankees, 2–0, in the opener before the Yankees won the next three. The Mets ran into even less resistance, winning the first two games in St Louis and arriving home filled with confidence the series would not return to the Midwest.

"Really, the Cardinals didn't bring their 'A' game," Mets catcher Todd Pratt says. "It was almost like after that first game—we're like, really, we're better than them. We're better than them."

The Cardinals did strike back for an 8–2 win in Game Three on October 14. The next day, with a chance to close out the Mariners, the Yankees fell, 6–2, in Seattle. The ALCS would return to New York after a travel day, which meant if the Mets could win Games Four and Five, they would be the first team to punch a Subway Series ticket.

The Mets gave up two first-inning runs in Game Four but scored four times in the bottom half and never trailed again on their way to a 10–6 win. Before Game Five, a certain giddy anticipation had begun to set in at Shea Stadium: the Mets were going to the World Series, and it sure would be nice if the Yankees joined them there.

"Anywhere I went today, I felt the electricity and the excitement," Mets coowner Fred Wilpon told *Newsday* prior to Game Five. "I don't know how many times I was asked, 'Do you want a Subway Series?'

"I said, 'I sure do.'"

The Mets wasted no time doing their part in Game Five, when they scored three times in the first and ended any doubt in the fourth, when Todd Zeile ripped a three-run double.

"Probably one of my most memorable moments as a Met," Zeile says. "I doubled with the bases loaded off the wall, got to second base, and they started playing 'Who Let The Dogs Out?' at like 80,000 decibels. The whole stadium was rocking, and I was like, that was it we're going to the World Series. I just remember the ground literally shaking to 'Who Let The Dogs Out?'"

Mike Hampton, who opened the series by throwing seven scoreless innings, locked up NLCS MVP honors by throwing a three-hit shutout in the 7–0 win. The Cards' Rick Wilkins, who was one of the catchers the Mets had employed before acquiring Mike Piazza on May 21, 1998, made the final out.

Timo Perez jumped up in center field while waiting for the ball to come down. Robin Ventura lifted Hampton as Piazza attempted to wrap them both in a bear hug. After mobbing one another, the Mets ran around Shea Stadium, slapping hands with fans reaching over the railings as "Who Let The Dogs Out?" pounded out of the speakers.

Both during and after the riotous celebration, the Mets were unified in one message.

"I think we felt like, hey, we can beat this team," Zeile says. "Matter of fact, I can remember sitting in the clubhouse, watching the Yankees playing for their berth and us all saying, sort of collectively, this is who we want. We want them to win. We want the Subway Series, and we want to try to take a piece of New York back."

For a few innings the next night, it appeared the Mariners might spoil the hopes of both New York teams and fans for a game, if not longer. The Mariners scored twice apiece in the first and fourth and carried a 4–3 lead into the seventh.

But Jose Vizcaino and Derek Jeter sandwiched singles around a bunt by Chuck Knoblauch to bring up David Justice, who hit 20 homers after being acquired from the Indians on June 29. The Mariners countered with veteran left-handed reliever Arthur Rhodes, who'd allowed a run in just two of his 14 postseason appearances.

"I just remember thinking I've got to get the run in from third to tie the game up," Justice says. "We tie the game up, then we're back 0–0 and we're at home; we'll have momentum."

Justice knew he had the momentum once he worked the count to 3–1 against Rhodes.

"I knew he had to come, he had to throw a fastball," Justice says. "I just couldn't miss it. So I just told myself, just shorten up, try to put a good swing on it, but don't try to hit him deep. Just hit a line drive."

Justice didn't hit a line drive. He did swing at a fastball down the middle and crushed it to right field, where the Mariners' Raul Ibanez barely moved. The ball landed in the upper deck.

A sellout crowd of 56,598 roared. The comeback was complete. The Subway Series countdown was back on.

Justice was no stranger to seismic postseason homers—his solo shot in Game Six of the 1995 World Series provided the only run as the Braves won their first championship since moving to Atlanta—but he understood the enormity of the moment. After gazing into the Yankees dugout, he raised his right fist as he neared first base and then pumped his left arm as he trotted between first and second.

"Soon as I hit it, I knew it was gone," Justice says. "And I remember looking at the dugout real fast, because I wanted to see the reaction of my teammates getting all excited, and they did. And then I just remember running around the bases and having a hard time running around the bases because it felt like an earthquake. It felt like the stadium was moving. And then you see all the people standing up and the beer everywhere. That was an exciting moment."

As Justice neared third base, Yankees radio play-by-play man Michael Kay, a native of the Bronx, summed up what was about to happen.

"Get your tokens ready!" Kay yelled. "You might be boarding the subway!"

The Yankees scored three more times in the inning. The Mariners scored three in the eighth off Orlando Hernandez and Mariano Rivera, but the outcome was never really in doubt, even with Rivera's fellow future Hall of Famer, Edgar Martinez, at the plate with two outs in the ninth.

Rivera threw one of his patented cut fastballs, and Martinez grounded to short. Derek Jeter charged and threw him out. It was 12:17 in the morning of October 18, and for the first time in 44 years, the Subway Series was happening.

"Start spreading the news!" NBC play-by-play man Bob Costas said. "New York, New York!"

Unlike a night earlier across town, there would be no victory laps by the Yankees, nor any bouncing up and down to the beat of the most popular song of the moment. The Yankees celebrated in their dignified, restrained style, exchanging enthusiastic hugs as Frank Sinatra's victorious version of "New York, New York" filled the stadium.

For while the Yankees had been here before—three straight times, four times in five years, and 37 times overall—everyone in and out of uniform knew what awaited baseball's preeminent franchise.

"I think it was our worst nightmare to play the Mets," Joe Torre says.

No one knew it at the time, but the Yankees and Mets were going to spend almost as much time waiting to begin the World Series as they would actually playing it. Just shy of 92 hours elapsed between Rivera retiring Martinez in the early minutes of October 18 and Andy Pettitte throwing the first pitch to Timo Perez at Yankee Stadium on October 21.

And since this is New York, the time before the World Series began was almost as interesting as the World Series itself.

The buildup of nearly four days allowed the dueling fan bases plenty of opportunity to exchange barbs as well as spend their disposable income on Subway Series memorabilia.

"You go to the dry cleaners, you go to the grocery store, and that's all they're talking about," Torre says. "That's what you can't hide from. So I think that ratcheted everything up."

*Newsday* reported a pair of local T-shirt printers—Apsco Enterprises in Brooklyn and Mart-Tex on Long Island—were producing hundreds of thousands of Subway Series shirts, which were almost literally flying off the shelves of local sporting goods stores.

"We are almost dead from all the running around that we have been doing," Kevin Williams, the general manager of a Modell's Sporting Goods in Valley Stream on Long Island, told *Newsday*. "People are taking the stuff out of the boxes as we are opening them."

The news cycle was a 24/7 beast by 2000, but the concept of consuming media in 140- or 280-character soundbites on a cell phone was still a decade away. So there were lots of inches to fill in local newspapers and lots of space to fill on the radio and television airwaves.

Just ask Mets first baseman Todd Zeile, who appeared on *Late Night With Conan O'Brien* and was interviewed alongside the Baha Men on *Good Morning America*, or outfielder Benny Agbayani, who was squired around the city on October 19 appearing on Howard Stern's radio show and on the national syndicated talk show hosted by Regis Philbin.

The other guests on the latter show: vice presidential candidate Joe Lieberman and Victoria Beckham, better known as "Posh Spice" from the Spice Girls.

"Leno next week," Mets public relations director Jay Horwitz said in the locker room, per *Newsday*. "Then *Crossfire* is trying to get him on."

In real time, Agbayani thought his biggest worry was Stern's famously profane line of questioning. (Agbayani said no, he had not dated Miss Hawaii and no, the Mets never showered with Bobby Valentine.) As it turned out, though, his answers to the actual baseball questions were the ones that would generate the headlines.

Both Stern and Philbin asked Agbayani who would win the World Series. And both times, Agbayani replied the Mets, in five games.

The next day, Agbayani spent an hour defending his statements to reporters in the Mets' locker room. At the end of the session, teammate and close friend Jay Payton walked by Agbayani's locker and made the zipping motion across his lips.

But the Mets were far more amused with the hubbub generated by Agbayani's comments than annoyed by his words.

"What the heck is wrong with that?" Mike Piazza said. "What's he going to predict? We're going to lose? If we're not confident we're going to win the Series, we shouldn't be here, no matter how you spin it. It'd be another thing to say it would be easy. That's trash-talking."

Agbayani expressed no regrets in 2019.

"What could I say?" Agbayani says. "I was a young guy; I believed in my team. That's how confident I was. I wasn't saying that out of cockiness. I just said it because I'm not going to let my teammates down. I believed in everybody else, and they believed in me.

"If I said something else, I would have got some looks in the clubhouse."

The Subway Series even made its way into the presidential election pitting George W. Bush against Al Gore. The two men made their final joint pre-Election Day appearance at the Al Smith Foundation Dinner in New York City on October 19. Bush, who as the owner of the Texas Rangers in 1992 was the man who dismissed future Mets manager Bobby Valentine, said he ". . . appreciate[d] the fact that he's going to vote for me even though I fired him."

Bush also delivered a dig at outgoing First Lady Hillary Rodham Clinton, who was running for senator in New York, and declared she was a Yankees fan even though she'd grown up a Cubs fan in suburban Chicago.

"There's really no place like New York," Bush said. "Especially for baseball fans like me and Mrs. Clinton."

The Yankees, meanwhile, were doing their best to stay off the front and back pages. While the Mets, who had only three players with World Series experience, were wide-eyed and exuberant, the Yankees carried themselves with a weary, been-there-done-that demeanor.

Eleven players on the 2000 team had been a part of the 1996, 1998, and 1999 World Series winners.

In this regard, the Yankees were taking their cue from owner George Steinbrenner, who never accepted defeat and already couldn't conceive of the possibility the Yankees' dynasty would be derailed by the Mets—*the Mets!*

"There was a significant amount of pressure that you didn't want to lose the Subway Series," former Yankees media relations director Rick Cerrone says. "When I show people my 2000 ring, they say, 'Wow, that's beautiful.' Yeah, it was either get this, or you're fired."

With a laugh, Cerrone added he wasn't serious. Still, imagine the Mets winning the World Series and a forever-trampled fan base rising and declaring its supremacy. Imagine a Mets victory serving as a baseball coup in the Big Apple. Imagine the headlines in the papers.

"I think George was concerned with the Mets—definitely that was a big part of it," says David Cone, who played for the Mets from 1987 until 1992 and was a member of all four Yankees championship teams. "George was relentless. It was always next. You've got to win again. The day after we win a World Series, he's got meetings going on about next year. The Mets were a big part of that.

"George was obviously keen on the battle for the back page, and the Mets were direct competition."

While Steinbrenner was usually a ubiquitous presence in celebratory locker rooms, he was nearly invisible following the Yankees' ALCS-clinching win over the Mariners. The only time he was sighted in the clubhouse, he was walking out in an entourage that included New York City Mayor Rudolph Giuliani. The Mets, clearly, were already on his mind.

"There was more pressure against the Mets, I would say, than [against] some of the other teams, if that could possibly be in a World Series," Yankees outfielder Paul O'Neill says. "Seldom do you go into a World Series with, I don't want to say nothing to gain, but little to gain and everything to lose. We were expected to win.

"And if we didn't then we were going to pay for it from fans, media, everything. Mr. Steinbrenner made it apparent that we were not going to lose to the Mets."

Steinbrenner, who never met a headline he didn't like, also declined interview requests as the World Series approached. His silence said it all: Sure, the Yankees had won the last two championships and three of the last four. By any measure, they were baseball's newest dynasty. And none of it would matter if they didn't win four games from the Mets.

"You can't lose to the Mets," Cerrone says. "You can't lose that Series. You can't. You can't!"

Even before the first Subway Series pitch in 44 years was finally thrown, there was evidence the long-awaited Yankees-Mets clash would not resonate nearly as loudly outside the five boroughs.

Small-to-mid-market teams won the first five championships of the 1990s: The Cincinnati Reds, Minnesota Twins, Toronto Blue Jays (who won back-to-back titles in 1992 and 1993), and Atlanta Braves. But the Yankees began reasserting New York's baseball dominance by winning three of the four titles from 1996 through 1999, and the idea of watching both Big Apple teams in the World Series seemed too much to bear for the rest of the country.

The ratings for each League Championship Series were off by more than 30 percent from the previous season. The ALCS drew a 7.7 rating on NBC, while the NLCS drew a 6.2 rating on FOX.

"Just being around the city and walking the streets—you always see a lot of Yankee gear on the streets where we stay downtown, it was just as much Mets stuff for the first time in a long time," says Arizona Diamondbacks broadcaster Bob Brenly, who served as an analyst for FOX during the World Series. "So we had the feeling going in that this was going to be something special at least here in New York.

"Now, as far as the rest of the country, yeah, I think there was a sentiment of 'Aww, geez, enough already. We see the Yankees every year.' Highlight game, whether it's Sunday night or Monday night or whatever we had going back then, it was the Yankees all the time."

To which New Yorkers in and out of uniform responded: So what?

"My opinion, this is the greatest city ever," Yankees reliever Jeff Nelson says. "When we played in 2000 in the World Series, I don't think the rest of the United States cared. But I thought it was the greatest. To watch the news, go to a sporting good shop and buy some memorabilia for the Subway Series—it was always a blast."

***

There was no red carpet rolled out at Yankee Stadium, though there was little doubting the World Series opener was the center of not only the sporting universe, but also the entertainment world.

Crowds several people deep lined the players' entrance to the Stadium several hours before first pitch. In keeping with the theme of the week, the Mets were much more wide-eyed and outwardly enthusiastic about the chaos awaiting them.

"I'm just really trying to enjoy it, not trying to put any greater emphasis on any one moment," Valentine said. "Because you never know what's going to happen."

While the normally publicity-hungry Steinbrenner marched into the Stadium without comment, Darryl Hamilton and Todd Zeile exited the Mets team bus toting camcorders, hoping to chronicle every moment they might otherwise miss in real time.

The most amusing moment preserved by Zeile?

"My son, Garrett, was in the cop car in front of us," Zeile says. "He was seven and they let him ride. We had a police escort. And he got on the mike when the Mets pulled up, and there were a lot of very adamant and dedicated Yankees fans. And he was like, 'Yankees suck, Yankees suck.' So they were like, 'Who is this?' And this little kid comes out in a Zeile jersey.

"So I wanted to get that, sort of encapsulate that."

Inside the stadium, the A-listers such as Giuliani, actor Billy Crystal, music power couple Puff Daddy and Jennifer Lopez, and the stars of various FOX shows (who can forget *Boston Public* debuted on the off-night in between Game One and Game Two?) were visible on the field, in the box seats, in the clubhouses, and even in the dugouts.

"It was just such a parade of Who's Who," Mets reliever Turk Wendell says. "Celebrities and the mayor. It was awesome to meet a lot of people in the limelight. Coming off the field in Game One and Sarah Jessica Parker is screaming at me above the dugout, begging me to sign a baseball for her. And I'm going, wow, can you sign one for me or have [husband] Matthew Broderick sign one? That was pretty cool."

Pop star Billy Joel, a Long Island native getting ready to sing the National Anthem, watched batting practice from the Mets' dugout and established himself as one of the few people who could get away with saying he was rooting for both teams.

"The last time, I remember I was a Brooklyn Dodgers fan," Joel said. "I was a little kid, then Brooklyn left and broke my heart and I switched to the Yankees. I was so mad, I switched leagues.

"And the Mets came along and they're a Long Island team. So I'm thrilled."

Mets reliever and lifelong New Yorker John Franco walked by.

"Hey, nice to see you," Franco said to Joel.

Another player walked by and wished Joel good luck.

"Hey, good luck to you, too," Joel said.

Joel was just shy of 10 months removed from what appeared to be the crowning moment of his career, performing at New York's Madison Square Garden as the clock struck midnight on New Year's Eve 1999. But he had to pause when asked if singing the Star-Spangled Banner before the first Subway Series game since 1956 was better than ringing in Y2K.

"I don't know yet," Joel said. "I had to wait until after the night of New Year's Eve to really know what it was. And I think after this series is over and all the hoopla's died down then I'll be able to weigh in.

"Right now, I'm just thrilled to be here."

Technological advancements and the concept of game presentation made those sitting in their living rooms in the tristate area and around the country feel far closer to the Subway Series action than they did 44 years earlier.

*Newsday* reported FOX planned to plant 75 microphones at Yankee Stadium and Shea Stadium to go along with the 22 cameras and five "super slo-mo video replay machines."

Fans at home got to see Joel's rendition of the National Anthem, which he performed as a bald eagle soared over the Stadium. Viewers also got a decidedly modern montage narrated by Crystal, who displayed his appreciation of New York baseball history and his knack for voice impersonations (along with a couple scenes from his recent movie, *Analyze This*) that aired shortly prior to first pitch.

"It's either New York or New York!" Crystal said. "Either way, we win!"

Any ceremonial first pitches in 1956 weren't as momentous as the one that preceded the Yankees-Mets opener, when Don Larsen and Yogi Berra provided one more chance for the Yankees to remind the Mets of their status as baseball's most decorated and charmed team.

Larsen's first pitch to Berra conjured up memories of October 8, 1956, and the most iconic moment in Subway Series history: Larsen's strikeout of the Dodgers' Dale Mitchell to complete the only perfect game in postseason history. The gem was the defining moment during a decade-long span in which two of New York's passions—mass transit and baseball—were merged on an almost annual basis.

But the two entities were not always, pardon the pun, traveling along the same path.

New York's first subway opened October 27, 1904, when 150,000 people paid five cents apiece to ride along the 9.1-mile stretch of track dubbed the "Manhattan Main Line."

Seven months earlier, Giants owner John T. Brush declared his National League team would never play its intracity rival, the American League's Highlanders (who would become the Yankees in 1912), even if the two squads advanced to the World Series. The Giants won the pennant while the Highlanders finished second, 1 ½ games behind the Boston Americans. But the World Series was not played because the Giants had no interest in playing the champion of what they considered to be the inferior league.

The World Series resumed the next year, when the Giants beat the Philadelphia Athletics in five games. But the American League got the last laugh: the next five times a New York team won the NL pennant, it lost to the AL representative.

By 1921, when the first Subway Series took place, more than a billion people per year were traveling the New York subways. The Polo Grounds and Yankee Stadium, located only a five-minute walk and one subway stop apart, welcomed 269,977 fans to the best-of-nine battle in which the Giants finally ended the drought of New York-based NL teams by beating the Yankees in eight games (1921 marked the third year in a four-year span where the Series was a best-of-nine affair).

The first of three consecutive Giants-Yankees clashes in the World Series—the Yankees finally won it all in 1923—also marked the start of a three-decade run in which New York dominated October. A Big Apple team made the World Series 27 times between 1922 and 1958. Thirteen times in that span, the World Series was a New York-New York affair. Cartoonist Willard Mullin coined the term "Subway Series" in 1941, when the Yankees beat the Brooklyn Dodgers in five games.

The Yankees won a record five straight World Series—bettering the mark set by the 1936–39 Yankees—from 1949 through 1953, a span in which they defeated the Dodgers three times and the Giants once.

Even when the Yankees' run ended, the championship still resided in New York. The Giants, buoyed by Willie Mays's legendary back-to-the-plate catch robbing Vic Wertz of an extra-base hit in the series opener, won their first title in more than 20 years when they swept the Cleveland Indians in 1954. The next year, "next year" finally came for the Dodgers, who beat the Yankees in seven games to win the franchise's first championship in eight tries.

The Subway Series era ended with a return to the norm in 1956, when the Yankees outlasted the Dodgers in seven games. Two years later, the Dodgers and Giants made the most seismic moves in baseball history when they began the sport's westward expansion by moving to Los Angeles and San Francisco, respectively.

The Yankees, meanwhile, just kept making the World Series—seven more from 1957 through 1964, though they won "just" three. Those were the final titles of the 10 earned by Berra, a record unmatched in baseball and exceeded in American sports only by the 11 rings collected by Boston Celtics center Bill Russell.

Berra retired after the 1963 season and was immediately named the Yankees' manager. But despite leading them to the World Series in his first year at the helm, Berra was fired by general manager Ralph Houk, who declared Berra was not yet ready to be a big-league skipper.

Berra was no longer a member of the Yankees, but his status as the fabric of New York baseball remained unchanged. The fledgling Mets hired Berra as a coach for the 1964 season, when he actually came out of retirement to play four games for the team before returning full-time to the bench. He was a coach on the miracle 1969 World Series-winning team and the manager in 1973, when the Mets made the playoffs with an 82–79 record but won the pennant and pushed the dynastic Oakland Athletics to seven games in the World Series.

Watching the Mets turn from lovable losers into champions provided Berra a unique perspective on the differences between the franchises and their expectations.

"My grandmother always used to say this really funny thing," says Lindsay Berra, the oldest grandchild of Yogi and Carmen Berra. "She was like, 'We had a great time with the Yankees because we won a lot. But we didn't know what real fun was until we joined the Mets.'"

Berra was fired by the Mets in 1975 and rejoined the Yankees as a coach in 1976, when the Yankees returned to the World Series for the first time since Berra's lone season as manager. He was on the staff for the 1977 and 1978 World Series champions as well as for the 1981 club, which fell to the Dodgers in six games.

Remarkably, the Mets' World Series win in 1986 marked the first time a New York baseball team made the World Series without Berra in uniform—as either a player, coach, or manager—since 1945, a span in which the Yankees and Mets combined to make 21 appearances in the Fall Classic.

And even in 1986, there was a Berra connection: to get to the World Series, the Mets had to beat the Houston Astros, whose bench coach was . . . Yogi Berra, who was thousands of miles from the Big Apple and wearing the Astros' garish rainbow uniform because he'd promised never to set foot in Yankee Stadium again as long as the team was owned by George Steinbrenner. It was Steinbrenner who had hired Berra as manager in 1984 but fired him just 16 games into the 1985 season.

Berra was less upset over being fired than he was by the fashion in which he was fired by Steinbrenner, who had general manager Clyde King deliver the news.

And for more than a decade, Berra's forgiveness was the one thing Steinbrenner could neither purchase nor obtain. But the relationship was mended with an in-person visit to Berra's museum in New Jersey—arranged by Yankees radio reporter Suzyn Waldman—and an apology by Steinbrenner to Berra in January 1999.

"Fourteen years, I'd say, is long enough," Berra told reporters afterward. "He apologized again."

"It was a stupid thing on my part," Steinbrenner said. "Sometimes, it takes a long time to get things right."

Afterward, Cerrone saw an unusually content Steinbrenner.

"The happiest I ever saw George Steinbrenner was when we walked out of the Yogi Berra Museum and drove back to the Stadium," Cerrone says. "That's the happiest I ever saw him.

"Because his World Series euphoria lasted about an hour."

Berra was officially welcomed back to Yankee Stadium with Yogi Berra Day on July 18, 1999, when he caught the first pitch from Larsen. Hours later, David Cone threw a perfect game as the Yankees beat the Montreal Expos.

And now, 15 months later, Berra was back, a symbol of Subway Series history and the Yankees' dominance in New York's intracity baseball battles as well as his status as the one person who could bridge two vastly different franchises and their battling fan bases.

"Grandpa was the most black-and-white, forthright, morally direct person you will ever meet," Lindsay Berra says. "There were no shades of gray with the way he viewed the world. There wasn't any nuance. OK, he was a Yankee for a little while. He was a Met for a little while. So what's the problem? He wouldn't read into the rivalry, the this side of town, the that side of town, I was born here, you were born there, I don't talk to you during baseball season. That would all just be so ridiculous. He would literally thumb his nose at that.

"I think he looked back very fondly on his time with the Yankees and he looked back very fondly [on] his time with the Mets and it would never occur to him that it was an odd thing or that he shouldn't have fun with both teams or that you could be a part of both teams."

After Berra caught Larsen's first pitch, it was time for the next, long-awaited Subway Series chapter to be penned. As FOX broadcaster Joe Buck noted in his opening comments prior to Game One, the Subway Series was a familiar topic in baseball history, but one about to be experienced for the first time by millions of people—including Buck himself, who was born 13 years after the previous Subway Series.

"Well, it's exciting for all of us to introduce to a new generation of fans across the country, myself included, something that we all heard about growing up from parents, from grandparents, a time when the World Series meant two New York titans clashing in October.

"It took 44 years, but the Subway Series is back."

Finally, at 8:13 p.m., after days of hysteria, it was time for baseball to begin. In a showdown that embodied the different paths the Yankees and Mets took to the World Series, homegrown "Core Four" ace Andy Pettitte fired a first pitch strike to Mets leadoff hitter Timo Perez, who was in the minor leagues just weeks earlier.

The Subway Series was finally underway. But the hype and hoopla were just beginning.

***

Pettitte and Al Leiter matched zeroes for the first five innings, though it didn't take nearly that long to set the tone for the series.

The bottom of the second inning ended with Yankees third baseman Scott Brosius hitting a slow roller up the first base line. The ball was fielded by Todd Zeile, who held his glove out for what appeared to be the routine tag. But Brosius lowered his shoulders and barreled into Zeile, who hung onto the ball.

Zeile had no problem with Brosius's effort in real time ("Play the game hard, and sometimes there's contact, sometimes there's hit by pitches, sometimes you slide hard into a guy"), nor even in retrospect. But it did symbolize the uniqueness of this World Series.

"I think we felt like this was a battle, this was a war," Zeile says. "These were teams that were familiar with each other. These were teams that—even though the rivalry was fueled as much by the media as it really was by the guys on the team—we had the Clemens-Piazza thing as the lingering fuel for it. So it made it even more of a spectacle on a bigger stage."

A less forceful but no less foreboding tone was set over the first six innings by the Mets, who went down against Pettitte in order in the first before putting the leadoff batter on in each of the next five frames. But the Mets found increasingly ominous ways not to score against a team well known for capitalizing on the tiniest of mistakes.

Zeile was stranded at first following a single in the second. Todd Pratt was hit by a pitch in the third and left at second. Mike Piazza was picked off first after singling in the fourth. After Benny Agbayani doubled in the fifth, Jay Payton didn't run out a dribbler that landed just in front of the plate, where Jorge Posada picked up the ball and tagged Payton.

Then came the sixth inning.

Perez singled before Pettitte retired Edgardo Alfonzo and Piazza. Pettitte was one strike away from escaping the inning in uneventful fashion when Zeile crushed a pitch to deep left field. Off the bat, it looked like the Mets were about to take a 2–0 lead. Perez thought so too and slowed down as he rounded second base. For a split second, Zeile raised his fist as he rounded first base believing the ball was gone.

So did most of the people in the opposing dugout.

"I thought when he first hit it, it was a home run," Joe Torre said afterward.

Except the ball didn't clear the fence. It landed atop the left field wall and rolled along the padding for a few feet. Had it fallen backward, Zeile would have had his two-run homer. But it fell forward and onto the warning track, where David Justice picked the ball up and fired toward the infield.

Perez had sped up by this point and reached third base in a full sprint. Justice's throw was cut off by shortstop Derek Jeter, who, in one motion, caught the ball, whirled, and threw home. The ball beat Perez and was caught by Posada, who applied the tag to end the inning as a bewildered Zeile stood at second base.

"Right on the money, an off-balance throw to get Perez," FOX analyst Tim McCarver said. "Wow."

The surreal sequence of events continued building two more legends: the Yankees' reputation as a ruthless machine ready to pounce on any minor mistake by an opponent and the idea of Yankee Stadium as a place where the home team was aided by borderline supernatural forces.

"We were lined up perfectly for a relay," Yankees first base coach Lee Mazzilli says. "You could very easily just shut the play down. But 'Jeets' didn't shut the play down. We played it out. And it was a mistake on their part. You're not supposed to umpire; you let the umpires umpire and you play the game. And it worked in our favor."

Everything about the play was agonizingly familiar to Zeile, who was a member of the Baltimore Orioles during Game One of the 1996

AL Championship Series when 12-year-old Yankees fan Jeffrey Maier reached over the right field wall and caught a fly ball by Jeter before the Orioles' Tony Tarasco could catch it.

Despite the interference, right field umpire Rich Garcia ruled Jeter hit a tie-breaking homer. The Yankees went on to win Game One in 11 innings and took the ALCS in five games. As for Zeile's near homer four years later . . .

"It's one of those things that I think some people still have created this fiction around the fact that if there was replay, it would be a home run," Zeile says. "But, I mean, it is what it is, right? And it was sort of a defining moment, that sort of part of the whole rivalry between the Mets and the Yankees that, like, the Yankees are the dynasty organization that finds a way to get on the good side of that one and not have that [happen].

"I'd already experienced it."

And Zeile, who would play 16 seasons for 11 teams and collect more than 2,000 hits, had just experienced his defining moment.

"People, invariably, when I come to New York or when I come to the ballpark, I walk down the street, somebody sees me—there's quite often a reference to Timo Perez," Zeile says. "Looking back, it was the difference, potentially the difference, in the game."

"That's the play that I'm probably most asked about."

The Yankees didn't wait long to make the Mets pay for Perez's mistake. With Yankee Stadium still buzzing from the chaotic end to the top half of the inning, Vizcaino led off the home half of the sixth with an infield single. Vizcaino went to second on a bunt by Chuck Knoblauch before Jeter walked.

David Justice followed with a two-run double to deep left-center field to give the Yankees the lead and provide the reminder McCarver was about to share with the rest of the country.

"Once again, you do not give the Yankees this type of opening," McCarver said. "The Mets have been terrible on the bases all night, and finally the Yankees took advantage of them."

With nine outs to go, the task was tall for the Mets. The Yankees had not given up the lead in a playoff game they led after the fifth inning since Game Four of the 1997 AL Division Series, when, with the Yankees four outs away from eliminating the Cleveland Indians and advancing to the AL Championship Series, Mariano Rivera gave up a game-tying home run to Sandy Alomar. The Indians earned a walk-off win in the ninth and won the decisive Game Five.

But the Mets were not about to go down so easily and required just one out to tie the game and two outs to take the lead. Robin Ventura led off the seventh by popping out, after which Agbayani and Payton singled and Todd Pratt walked to load the bases. Bobby Valentine sent up Bubba Trammell, who was hitless in three playoff at-bats but was 7-for-18 with a home run against Pettitte, to pinch-hit for shortstop Mike Bordick. Trammell rewarded Valentine by delivering a two-run single.

After Perez bunted the runners over, Joe Torre pulled Pettitte for Jeff Nelson. The first batter he faced was Edgardo Alfonzo, who, on a night previously filled with baserunning gaffes by the Mets, legged out an infield single to third base as Pratt scored the go-ahead run.

Now, all of a sudden, it was the Mets who were nine outs away from a stunning victory.

"We had a 2–0 lead in the seventh inning, and that's usually our strong point," Torre said afterward. "But they wouldn't let that happen."

Leiter worked around a one-out single in the bottom of the seventh, Nelson threw a perfect top of the eighth, and John Franco—the lifelong New Yorker finally making his World Series debut at the age of 40—allowed a single in a scoreless bottom of the inning.

The Mets were three outs away from victory. Torre, looking to keep the Yankees within a run, brought in Rivera for the ninth, but the Mets nearly dented the dominant closer for an insurance run. Pratt was hit by a pitch with one out before Kurt Abbott, who replaced Bordick at shortstop, doubled.

With the infield drawn in, Perez followed with a grounder that bounced over the glove of a leaping Rivera. Vizcaino, positioned right behind Rivera, moved in for the ball, which bounced up and off his chest. The slow-footed Pratt, who wasn't running on contact with one out, took two steps toward home as the ball squirted loose but headed back to the bag as Vizcaino recovered, picked up the ball, and fired to first, where his throw got Perez by a step.

In the booth, McCarver second-guessed the decision not to send Pratt. Nearly two decades later, Pratt admitted he wonders if he should have bolted home once the ball got beyond Rivera.

"I kind of hesitated a little bit because I didn't think I could make it," Pratt says. "Looking back on it, maybe if I would have gotten a better read on the ball. I thought it was going to Mo."

Rivera struck out Alfonzo to escape the jam and send the game to the bottom of the ninth, where Armando Benitez would try to close out the Yankees and hand them their first World Series loss in exactly three years.

But Benitez's history in the playoffs and against the Yankees was decidedly spotty. He entered the World Series with five blown saves in eight postseason chances and seven homers allowed, the latter of which was the most in history. Among the homers he served up: Jeter's fan-aided round-tripper in the 1996 ALCS.

Less than two years later, Benitez touched off perhaps baseball's fiercest brawl of the decade. Benitez, still pitching for the Orioles, gave up a go-ahead home run to Tim Raines in the eighth inning. He responded by plunking Tino Martinez on the back between the 2 and the 4 of his uniform number on his next pitch. Benitez was immediately ejected, and as the benches and bullpens emptied, he dropped his glove and raised his arms toward the Yankees' dugout.

The first punches were thrown by Yankees relievers Nelson and Graeme Lloyd. Benitez flailed at the pair of Yankees as the fracas carried over on to the edge of the Orioles dugout, where Darryl Strawberry reached across a crowd and tried to punch Benitez. Strawberry missed and fell into the dugout, and the momentum from the brawl carried dozens of players tumbling down the steps.

The brawl basically spelled the end of Benitez's tenure with the Orioles, who traded him to the Mets following the season. He rebuilt his reputation as a dominant set-up man in front of Franco in 1999 before taking over at closer after Franco missed two months with a finger injury.

But Benitez continued to struggle in the playoffs for the Mets, who were three outs away from becoming the first baseball team to ever force a seventh game in a series they trailed three games to none when they took a 9–8 lead in the 10th inning of Game Six of the 1999 NL Championship Series against the Atlanta Braves. But Benitez allowed the game-tying run in the bottom of the inning, and the Braves went on to win the pennant in the 11th.

In 2000, Benitez blew a save in Game Two of the NL Division Series by giving up a two-run home run to J.T. Snow, though the Mets scored in the 10th inning, and Franco closed the game out in the bottom of the inning.

As he took the mound late on a Saturday night in the Bronx, Benitez had a chance to render meaningless most of those implosions. All he had to do was set down the Yankees' sixth-, seventh-, and eighth-place hitters. Of course, those hitters were Jorge Posada, Paul O'Neill, and Scott Brosius, a trio that would bat in the middle of the order for just about anybody else.

Posada led off with a seven-pitch battle in which he fouled off a pair of 2–2 pitches before flying out to deep right-center field. Up stepped O'Neill, dubbed "The Warrior" by George Steinbrenner for his scorching intensity and ability to play through pain.

Unfortunately for O'Neill, that's exactly what he was doing down the stretch in 2000. The 37-year-old was battling a sore right hip and hit .222 in September before batting .231 in the Yankees' first 11 playoff games.

O'Neill was 1-for-3 in the World Series opener when he stepped into the box against Benitez, who fell behind 1–0 before O'Neill swung and missed at the second pitch and took a called strike two on Benitez's third offering.

"The Warrior" knew he was in trouble.

"Thing I remember about it is being down in the count and feeling like, I really don't have a chance here," O'Neill says. "I wasn't feeling good at the plate at the time."

O'Neill went into waste pitches mode, lunging across the plate and fouling Benitez's next two pitches into the seats beyond third base. He then took a pair of pitches to work the count full before reaching out and fouling off the next two pitches, both of which landed in the opposite field.

"You get behind in the count to a guy with that kind of stuff and just keep fouling balls off, fouling balls off," O'Neill says. "And as you're fouling them off, you're realizing, 'I'm not going to put a ball hard in play here.'"

Behind the plate, Pratt was just tired of seeing O'Neill put the ball anywhere but his mitt.

"It was just unbelievable," Pratt says. "I was like, 'C'mon, miss, miss!' But great at-bat by him."

Turns out O'Neill didn't have to put a ball in play anywhere. The 10th pitch of the at-bat was high and outside. Ball four.

"You're at such a disadvantage, behind in the count, that you'd do anything just to keep the at-bat going," O'Neill says. "You can't take a pitch and not give it a shot. That's what most of those foul balls were, just trying to stay in there."

The Yankees completed their game-tying rally in piecemeal fashion, though it seemed much faster to players on both sides. Within a span of six pitches, pinch-hitter Luis Polonia and Vizcaino each singled to load the bases. Knoblauch followed with a sacrifice fly. Benitez had his sixth postseason blown save—the first by a closer in the World Series since Jose Mesa squandered the lead for the Indians in Game 7 of the 1997 Fall Classic.

"I can remember fighting and fighting," O'Neill says. "And I remember ball four, and just how quick things happened after that."

Benitez struck out Jeter to end the ninth and send the game to extra innings. But the damage had been done, and a clear turning point in the World Series had been established.

"I was on the treadmill not too long ago working out and [watching] YES [Network] and here comes Game One," Zeile says. "They picked it up in the like the 10th or something, I'm like, God, I forgot that we—in my mind, it was the O'Neill at-bat, and in my mind, that's what ended the game because I think that at-bat became such a defining thing, when he scored to tie the game to send it into extra innings.

"I think that was when I probably shut some of the other pieces out."

To be fair, there wasn't much for Zeile to remember after the ninth, at least from the Mets' perspective. Rivera and Mike Stanton combined to set down all nine Mets from the 10th through the 12th. Midnight came and went, as did bedtimes for fans young and old throughout the tristate area.

"Tomorrow's Sunday," Joe Buck said on FOX. "A lot of late arrivals in church."

In New Jersey, future regular-season Subway Series participant Todd Frazier, then a 14-year-old high school freshman, had no problem negotiating a later bedtime.

"My Dad said, 'Go ahead, it don't matter,'" Frazier says.

The Yankees, meanwhile, inched closer to another trademark win of the dynasty era in a fashion that must have filled the Mets and their fans with a sense of impending doom.

The Yankees had runners on first and second with none out in the bottom of the 10th and loaded the bases with one out before Glendon Rusch entered for the Mets to face O'Neill. This time, there was no battle, and O'Neill hit into a double play.

In the 11th, Jose Vizcaino singled with one out. Derek Jeter drew a two-out walk, but ball four sailed past Pratt, and Jeter and Vizcaino advanced to second and third, respectively. Turk Wendell relieved Rusch and retired Glenallen Hill on a fly out to right.

Unfortunately for the Mets, Wendell, who began warming up in the sixth and estimated he went up and down ". . . probably five or six times," was already gassed.

"I was lucky to get out of the inning with Glenallen Hill popping up," Wendell says. "And I probably should have told Valentine, 'Look, I'm pretty much spent right now because I've been up so much.'"

Wendell laughed.

"But Game One of the World Series," he says.

With one out in the 12th, Tino Martinez beat out an infield single. Jorge Posada followed with a double to send Martinez to third. O'Neill was intentionally walked to bring up veteran utility infielder Luis Sojo, who had a track record of big hits in big situations.

Sojo had seven RBIs in the first two rounds of the playoffs and was most famous for delivering the biggest hit of the one-game playoff for the AL West title in 1995, when he laced a bases-clearing double in the seventh inning of the Seattle Mariners' 9–1 win.

In the on-deck circle, Vizcaino figured he had a far better chance of mobbing Sojo near first base than actually stepping to the plate.

"We saw who was hitting, so I wasn't even thinking that I was going to go up there to hit because I know what type of guy he is, and he always comes [up] clutch," Vizcaino says.

But Sojo popped up to Pratt. The only batter between the Mets and escaping a third straight jam was Vizcaino, who not only played for the Mets from 1994 until July 1996, but was also, at the time, one of just two players to play for all four teams that originated in New York. (Strawberry played for the Mets, Dodgers, Giants, and Yankees from 1983 through 1998, while Ricky Ledee would complete the cycle by 2006.)

The Yankees acquired Vizcaino in June to provide some second base insurance behind Knoblauch, who could no longer make an accurate throw to first base. Joe Torre started Vizcaino in the World Series opener because he was 10-for-19 against Al Leiter.

It was an assignment that initially filled Vizcaino with jitters. He says it was only the second time he'd ever been nervous prior to a big-league game, with the first being his major league debut with the Dodgers on September 10, 1989.

"When I walked to the field in the first inning, I was shaking; I was nervous," Vizcaino says. "I got traded over there because Chuck Knoblauch had the yips; he could not throw the ball to first base. So I would just have thoughts of that in my mind like, 'Oh please, don't do it, don't do it, don't do it.' And then I say why? You are good. So I started thinking positive things, and I was just praying that Timo Perez hit a ball to me."

Perez opened the game by grounding out to Vizcaino.

"He hit a ground ball to me, I throw to first and then it was just like a normal game," Vizcaino says.

Vizcaino went 1-for-3 against Leiter, but Torre kept him in the game despite having power-hitting options such as Hill and Jose Canseco on the bench. Vizcaino rewarded Torre's trust by singling against Benitez in the ninth and again against Rusch in the 11th.

And now the man who fielded the first out of the first Subway Series game in 44 years was going to deliver the winning hit.

"When I saw he popped up the ball, I said, well, this is my time, this is what I was dreaming when I was a kid: being in a World Series game and getting that game-winning hit," Vizcaino says. "And that's why I didn't waste any time. I knew he was going to throw me a first-pitch fastball."

Wendell's 20th pitch of the game—only he knows how many he actually threw before that in the bullpen—sailed over the plate. Vizcaino swung and laced a clean single to left field. Martinez trotted home with the winning run to end the longest game in World Series history at 12:54 a.m., a mere four hours and 51 minutes after it started.

"We had a resilient group, that's all I can say," Torre says. "We had been to the World Series every year but one [since 1996], so we were a pretty resilient group. They weren't going to be denied."

Vizcaino raised his fist as he neared first base. He touched the bag, turned, and was mobbed by teammates—led by Jeter—pouring out of the home dugout.

"I felt I was on top of the world, because you're going into the game knowing that everybody's watching," Vizcaino says.

It didn't feel quite so good for the Mets. After his fruitless pursuit of Vizcaino's hit, Mets left fielder Joe McEwing reached down for the ball and . . .

"The magnitude of that hit, catching it and knowing we just lost Game One," McEwing says. "And just turning around and throwing the ball in the upper deck, all in one motion. It seemed like all in one motion. I let it go. So that's still vivid."

Wendell, who grew up loathing the Yankees as a Red Sox fan in western Massachusetts, trudged off the field as the celebration roared behind him.

"The walk of shame off the field like that in Game One of the World Series is almost as devastating as losing the World Series altogether—the final out of the World Series," Wendell says. "That really sucked."

In the interview room a few minutes later, Bobby Valentine tried to lighten the mood.

"Well, we came in with very little World Series experience, and we got a lot of it in one night," Valentine said. "So . . . we're doing a good job in the experience category."

But nothing anyone had ever seen could have prepared the Yankees and the Mets for what would happen later that night in Game Two.

# CHAPTER 2
# GAME TWO

**Yankees 6, Mets 5**
**Yankees lead series, two games to none**

**THE WEIRDEST SEQUENCE** in the history of the World Series—or perhaps any type of championship series—lasted barely two minutes in the first inning of Game Two. One can only imagine that was more than enough time for Roger Clemens and Mike Piazza to see their complicated history flash before their eyes.

It was not, of course, nearly enough time to ponder the alternate timeline where the paths of Clemens and Piazza never crossed in a game of importance. But ponder all that had to happen for Clemens and Piazza to converge at all, and the possibility that two of the greatest to ever play their respective positions would have only met in informal situations at an All-Star Game, or perhaps while standing in solidarity at a press conference during a work stoppage.

Or imagine the alternate timeline where Clemens and Piazza are not foes but teammates, forming maybe the most potent battery in the history of the game as well as a friendship borne out of their similarly nondescript baseball upbringings and their ability to find fuel in slights, both real and perceived.

Roger Clemens and Mike Piazza. Teammates. Friends. Baseball's most potent 1-2 punch. How weird would that have been?

Could it have been any weirder than what actually happened?

***

Roger Clemens and Mike Piazza were born a little more than six years and 500 miles apart. While he forever built his reputation as a hard-throwing, no-nonsense Texan with the alliterative nickname "Rocket" naturally attached to "Roger," Clemens was actually born William Roger Clemens in Dayton, Ohio, on August 4, 1962, the fifth and final child of Bess and Bill Clemens.

Bess Clemens left her husband when her youngest child was five months old but soon met and married Woody Booher, whom Clemens would come to consider as his father figure. Booher moved the Clemens family into his luxurious house in Vandalia, Ohio, a home that included a pool and land on which six horses roamed. Clemens's serene childhood was shattered forever, though, when he was nine years old and Woody died of a heart attack at home.

Athletically, Clemens was viewed as an eager if only moderately talented baseball player who battled asthma as well as a doughy physique. One of his Little League coaches, Walter Peck, told Clemens biographer Jeff Pearlman that Clemens ". . . was short and fat. I had him on an all-star team, and he didn't even start. He simply wasn't good enough."

But Clemens was determined, and, motivated by high school coach Charlie Maiorana, he shed his baby fat, became enamored with fitness, and turned into the ace of the Spring Woods high school baseball team as a senior in 1980 even though his fastball barely reached the mid-80s. He also earned a reputation for meanness on the mound, often taunting or throwing at opposing hitters and once even firing a pickoff throw into the opponent's dugout.

Clemens went undrafted after graduating high school—though he did write in his autobiography of being drafted in the 22nd round by the Minnesota Twins and turning down their insulting offer—and traveled to tryouts around the country with a teammate looking to sign a free agent deal. With no offers forthcoming, he went to San Jacinto Junior College in Texas, where his fastball gained 10 mph thanks to the tutelage of head coach Wayne Graham.

His performance as a college freshman impressed the Mets, who selected him in the 12th round. Clemens threw for then-Mets Manager Joe Torre and Bob Gibson, the Mets pitching coach and Hall of Fame hurler known for his intensity on the mound and willingness to pitch inside. While Gibson wasn't impressed with what he saw, the Mets liked Clemens enough to offer him $25,000.

But in a sign of the hard-line negotiating tactics he would take throughout his career, Clemens refused to sign unless the Mets offered him several thousand dollars more. The Mets hoped to meet with Clemens and to try and change his mind, but each of the three summer league games scout Joe McIlvaine tried to attend was rained out. The Mets ended up using the money they had saved for Clemens on a fifth-round pick named Steve Phillips, who never got beyond Double-A before joining the team as an executive. Phillips eventually succeeded McIlvaine as general manager in 1997 and pulled off the blockbuster trade that brought Piazza to New York in May 1998.

Still, things worked out pretty well for Clemens. After turning down the Mets, Clemens signed with the University of Texas and helped the Longhorns to the national title in 1983, the same year he was drafted 19th overall by the Boston Red Sox.

At Texas and as a minor leaguer with the Red Sox, Clemens continued to become known as someone whose competitive streak and disdain for opposing batters often overwhelmed him on the mound.

According to *The Rocket That Fell to Earth*, Jeff Pearlman's biography of Clemens, the right-hander trash-talked Oklahoma State slugger Pete Incaviglia during the first inning of an NCAA Tournament game, yelling, "Fuck you guys! You guys aren't worth shit."

When asked by a teammate what he was doing, Clemens reportedly said, "Ah, fuck him, I'm just pumped up."

Clemens didn't stop at just words as his weapon a couple months later. In the midst of a brief stop with the Red Sox's Single-A affiliate in Winter Haven, Florida, Clemens took umbrage at Ronald Davis, a member of the Detroit Tigers' Lakeland affiliate, sliding hard into Mike Brumley, who also played with Clemens at Texas.

"You'll get yours, you son of a bitch!" Clemens yelled, per Pearlman's biography. "I'll see you in two fucking days!"

Two days later, Clemens struck out the first five Tigers he faced. Davis batted sixth. With his first pitch, Clemens threw a fastball that landed on Davis's skull. Davis tried charging the mound but got dizzy and fell over. While Davis was rushed to a local hospital, Clemens finished with 15 strikeouts and earned a promotion to Double-A New Britain.

"I understood him throwing at me," Davis told Pearlman. "I can respect standing up for a teammate. But he threw at my head. At my head! You don't mess with somebody's career like that."

Two days later, Clemens wrote Davis a letter apologizing and insisting he meant to hit him in the leg. It wasn't the last time Clemens would express remorse after a beanball incident.

Clemens didn't wait long to leave the minor leagues in his rearview mirror. He was in the Red Sox's rotation in 1984. After an injury-plagued 1985 season, Clemens won the Cy Young and Most Valuable Player Awards in 1986, when he went 24–4 and struck out a major league-record 20 batters against the Seattle Mariners on April 20.

By 1992, the season in which he turned 30, Clemens had won three Cy Youngs, four AL ERA crowns, and 152 games—more wins than recent 300-game winners Steve Carlton, Nolan Ryan, Don Sutton, Gaylord Perry, and Phil Niekro all had through the season in which they turned 30.

Still, despite the unqualified success and his Hall of Fame track, Clemens was not exactly a beloved figure in Boston. A bitter holdout following his Cy Young/MVP season wounded all parties involved.

Even by the standards of a pitcher on a Hall of Fame track, his ego was enormous. All four of his sons sported names beginning with "K." Clemens devoted four pages in his autobiography to detailing a visit with President Ronald Reagan during the 1986 season.

In keeping with the tradition of previous Red Sox greats such as Ted Williams, Clemens feuded with the media. The emotion he showed on the mound often spilled over into interviews with Clemens's attempts to explain why conditions should be improved for Red Sox players turning into a rant about how he and his teammates had to carry their own luggage.

And then there was the belief that for all his bravado, he had yet to back up his words or come up big in the biggest spots. In 1989, his fellow hard-throwing Texan Nolan Ryan plunked Jim Rice on the shoulder, to which, according to Pearlman's biography, Clemens responded, "All right, you want to play that, we'll play that." Ryan glared at Clemens, who didn't respond either with his mouth or his right arm.

The Red Sox won the AL East four times with Clemens, but he posted a 3.88 ERA and won just one of his nine postseason starts in Beantown. There was mystery surrounding his exit from the potentially decisive Game Six of the 1986 World Series, though manager John McNamara's contention that Clemens asked out due to a blister after seven innings and 134 pitches was angrily denied by not only Clemens, but also teammates Marty Barrett and Dave Stapleton.

In 1990, with the Red Sox down three games to none against the Oakland Athletics in the American League Championship Series, Clemens took the mound wearing eye black and Teenage Mutant Ninja

Turtle shoelaces and argued with home plate umpire Terry Cooney until Cooney finally ejected him in the second inning with the Red Sox down, 3–0. They would lose, 3–1.

Clemens appeared to be winding down by 1996. The 34-year-old, his waistline expanding and his velocity decreasing, completed the final season of a four-year deal in which he went 40–39 with a 3.77 ERA. Red Sox general manager Dan Duquette, who took over the position in 1994, offered Clemens a four-year, $22 million deal with the hopes he would, as Duquette said, ". . . finish his career as a Red Sox" while also laying the foundation ". . . to establish a relationship beyond his playing career."

But after being wined and dined throughout the free agency process, Clemens ended up signing a three-year, $24.75 million contract—the richest ever awarded to a pitcher—with the division rival Toronto Blue Jays, who had just come off back-to-back losing seasons.

"The Red Sox and our fans were fortunate to see Roger Clemens play in his prime, and we had hoped to keep him in Boston during the twilight of his career," Duquette said.

Fueled, at the very least, by Duquette's words, Clemens's twilight turned historic. He won back-to-back Cy Youngs in his two seasons for the Blue Jays, who finished last in 1997 and 22 games behind the dynastic Yankees in 1998.

Clemens made a triumphant return to Boston on July 12, 1997, when he struck out 16 batters over eight innings. He struck out the side in his final inning of work and punctuated the performance by walking off the field and glaring in the direction of the Fenway Park suite where Duquette watched most games.

But unhappy with pitching in anonymity and for a noncontender, Clemens demanded a trade following the 1998 season, along with a contract extension.

Blue Jays general manager Gord Ash offered Clemens around the league, but most teams, understanding Ash wasn't exactly dealing from a position of strength, made borderline insulting offers. Clemens's hometown team, the Houston Astros, was interested, but not in meeting Clemens's reported request for an extension totaling more than $27 million.

As spring training neared, it appeared Clemens would have to return to Toronto. But on February 18, 1999, the team that needed Clemens the least stepped up with a better offer than anyone else had made Ash, though still one that would probably get rejected in any fantasy baseball league.

The Yankees, fresh off a season in which they'd won 114 regular-season games and a second World Series in three years but never shy under owner George Steinbrenner about adding to their stable of stars, were willing to ship popular veteran starting pitcher David Wells, young second baseman Homer Bush, and useful reliever Graeme Lloyd to the Blue Jays in exchange for Clemens.

It was nowhere near an equal return for a five-time Cy Young Award winner, and sending Clemens to the defending champions was the very definition of helping the rich get richer. But what choice did Ash have? Eager to get out from the Clemens distraction, he agreed to the trade with his Yankees counterpart Brian Cashman.

Nobody knew it at the time, but the first domino in the most bizarre player rivalry of the 21st century had fallen.

***

Mike Piazza's childhood was far more idyllic than the one endured by Clemens. Born September 4, 1968, as the second of Vince and Veronica Piazza's five children (all boys), Piazza and his family lived in Phoenixville, Pennsylvania, a well-to-do suburb of Philadelphia.

While Vince Piazza was a self-made millionaire who thrived as a used-car dealer and real estate magnate, his true passion was baseball. When Mike was eleven, his Dad built an indoor batting cage behind the family's house so that his son could take batting practice year-round.

One of Vince's oldest friends was his cousin Tommy Lasorda, the longtime Los Angeles Dodgers manager who would allow Mike to serve as bat boy when the Dodgers visited the Philadelphia Phillies. While he'd eventually become known as the greatest-hitting catcher ever, Piazza was a better pitching prospect as a Little Leaguer.

"I actually threw for Tommy and Ron Peranowski, who was the pitching coach at the time," Piazza said during a 2000 interview. "They thought I had a real good chance of being a prospect as a pitcher [at] about thirteen or fourteen. And then when I got to be fifteen or sixteen, I gradually gave up pitching."

When Mike was sixteen, his Dad learned from a friend, Dodgers scout Ed Liberatore, that Ted Williams was going to appear at a local autograph show. Liberatore introduced Williams to the elder Piazza, and after the two hit it off, Vince invited Ted to the house the next day to watch his son hit. Williams was impressed by the younger Piazza, who requested Williams sign a copy of his book *The Science of Hitting*.

Williams's inscription read:

"To my friend Mike, from Ted Williams. Don't forget me. Someday I'll be looking for you to get tickets to a game. Your friend, Ted Williams."

Unfortunately for Piazza, scouts didn't initially share Williams's enthusiasm. Piazza, now a lumbering first baseman short on athleticism, went undrafted following a successful career at Phoenixville High School, where he broke the school home run record previously held by big leaguer Andre Thornton and batted more than .400 as a senior. He attended the University of Miami but had just one hit in nine at-bats as a freshman before transferring to Miami-Dade Community College.

"To be quite honest, when you play in Pennsylvania, I had like 17 games my senior year, those kids [at Miami] are playing 40 games and 50 games and so on and so forth," Piazza said during an interview in 2000. "So I was just very much inexperienced for the Division I college level. I just wasn't ready. I was probably better off going to a JUCO right off the bat."

After Piazza hit .364 at Miami-Dade, Lasorda asked the Dodgers to draft Piazza as a favor. The team spent its last pick—a 62nd-round selection; only 43 players were drafted after Piazza—on Piazza in June 1988 and didn't follow up with him until August, when Piazza paid his own way to Dodger Stadium for a workout.

The Dodgers were intrigued with Piazza's power display, and once Lasorda convinced the team's scouts that Mike was a catcher, he was offered $15,000 to sign. Little did the Dodgers know it was at least $15,000 more than Piazza would have been willing to accept.

"If he would have said, 'You have to pay me $15,000,' I would have said, 'Well, let's see, I have 10 grand in the bank and . . .'" Piazza told *Sports Illustrated* in 1993. "I said yes before he said 'thousand.' He could have said $15 and it wouldn't have mattered."

The following spring, Piazza was assigned to Salem, the Dodgers' short-season Single-A affiliate in the Northwest League. It was not a typical destination for up-and-coming prospects. Only one other member of the 1989 Salem squad—fellow catcher Hector Ortiz, a 35th-round pick in 1988—would reach the majors.

Piazza fared well enough in his debut season, during which he led Salem with eight homers in 57 games. The following winter, he committed to catching by becoming the only English-speaking player to travel to the Dodgers' academy for Latin American prospects in the Dominican Republic. Among the things he had to worry about off the field: tarantulas climbing into his bed. Upon returning to the States, Piazza was assigned to full-season Class-A Vero Beach, for whom he posted a .670 OPS—the third-lowest mark on the team among players who played at least 80 games.

Still, despite the unglamorous conditions of the minors and any struggles he experienced, Piazza spoke fondly of his minor league days. During an interview in 2000, he recalled the support he felt from family across the country and how that provided the foundation to pursue his big-league dreams.

"You know your brothers come visit, [they] hang out with you, my father would come by, flip you a hundred bucks every now and then, just spending money," Piazza said. "Mom always putting cookies and food in the mail. No matter what happens, I have a great family to fall back on. So it has a way of alleviating pressure on yourself and anxiety. It just has a way of really relaxing you and allowing you to go out and play well."

Piazza finally emerged as a prospect in 1991, when he was sent to Bakersfield, a lower full-season Single-A affiliate, and hit a team-high 29 homers. He had another big season in 1992, when he hit 23 homers between Double-A San Antonio and Triple-A Albuquerque before earning a promotion to the Dodgers in September. Piazza played regularly at catcher down the stretch and hit his first big-league homer against the San Francisco Giants on September 12.

The Dodgers allowed longtime starting catcher Mike Scioscia to depart as a free agent following the 1992 season. Piazza entered spring training in the midst of a four-way battle for the job and hit .478 with four homers during exhibition play. He didn't slow down much once the season started, hitting .318 with 35 homers and 112 RBIs on his way to unanimously winning the NL Rookie of the Year and placing ninth in the MVP voting.

Piazza seemed destined for a storybook career spent following in the footsteps of his unofficial godfather Lasorda, who had been with the Dodgers in some capacity since 1948. But the idea of Piazza following in Lasorda's footsteps was doomed almost from the start.

In his autobiography, *Long Shot*, Piazza wrote of the shame he felt in the fall of 1990, when he went to take batting practice at the Dodgers' Instructional League facility but was told the workout was only for top prospects Billy Ashley and Billy Lott. Wrote Piazza: "That told me exactly where I stood in the organization. After two years, I was still the sixty-second-round draft choice."

There was no ignoring Piazza after his historic performance as a rookie, but contract negotiations in the winter of 1993–94 would further divide the two sides. As a player with a little more than one year of service time, Piazza was not yet eligible for salary arbitration and thus at the mercy of the Dodgers, who could simply renew his contract at a below-market rate. Precedence was not on Piazza's side: his teammate and good friend, Eric Karros, won the Rookie of the Year in 1992 and played for a little more than $400,000 in 1993.

Piazza and his representatives wanted to negotiate a three-year deal and used Frank Thomas's contract as a template. Thomas signed a three-year deal worth $4.5 million following his second big-league season in 1991. The Dodgers initially turned down Piazza's request and said they would renew his contract, after which Piazza—frustrated the club had spent almost $2 million in the preceding months on international free agent Chan Ho Park and draft pick Ryan Luzinski, who played catcher—declared he would not report to spring training and stormed out of the meeting room.

The Dodgers and Piazza eventually agreed on a three-year deal worth $4.2 million that locked him up through 1996, his first season of arbitration eligibility. Piazza, batted .334 with 92 homers and 290 RBIs during the contract, a span in which he finished sixth, fourth, and second, respectively, in the National League Most Valuable Player balloting.

Despite his big numbers, contract negotiations for a new deal in January 1997 remained complicated—not only by the rancorous history between the team and Piazza, but by the announcement that the O'Malley family, which had owned the team since 1950, was planning to sell the franchise.

The Dodgers offered him another three-year contract, but Piazza chose to sign a two-year deal worth $15 million that would allow him to test free agency following the 1998 season.

Piazza looked like a sure bet to get the richest contract in history during a 1997 season in which he hit .362 with 40 homers and 124 RBIs—one of the greatest offensive performances ever authored by a catcher.

In the spring of 1998, Piazza and the Dodgers continued to discuss a potential long-term extension that would keep him from reaching the open market, but the protracted sale of the team to FOX led to a high-stakes game of telephone in which actual communication between the parties was minimal or nonexistent.

Piazza sensed the Dodgers were trying to turn public opinion against him—a plot, he believed, that included beloved broadcaster Vin Scully. In his autobiography, Piazza wrote that "Vin Scully was crushing me" during a season-opening slump and that fans who were unhappy with him ". . . were taking their cue from Scully."

But the lone extended exchange between Piazza and Scully was a KTLA interview conducted in spring training in which Scully asked Piazza if the negotiations were on his mind and if he had established an ultimatum with the Dodgers regarding a deadline for a new deal. That was the extent of the contract-related questioning from the famously folksy Scully, who also asked Piazza about the five stolen bases he recorded in 1997.

"As God is my judge, I don't get involved in these things," Scully told the *Los Angeles Times* after Piazza's autobiography was released in 2013. "I can't imagine I would ever put my toe in the water as far as a player and his negotiations."

FOX finally purchased the Dodgers on March 19, after which the Dodgers made their offer: six years and $76 million without a no-trade clause—well short of the seven years and $105 million with a no-trade clause Piazza wanted.

Both sides traded barbs in the press before Piazza announced in early April that he would no longer negotiate with the Dodgers and would play the season out before filing for free agency.

If only it were that simple.

On May 14, after going 0-for-4 in a loss to the Philadelphia Phillies, Piazza was told General Manager Fred Claire wanted to see him. The best-hitting catcher since Yogi Berra and Johnny Bench knew what this meant: he'd been traded.

And not only that, but he'd been shipped to baseball's version of Siberia, the dismantled Florida Marlins. The reigning World Series champions, in the midst of a teardown and eager to shed right fielder

Gary Sheffield's salary, dealt Sheffield and several other players to the Dodgers in exchange for Piazza and Todd Zeile.

Piazza later learned the blockbuster was pulled off at the executive level and involved much more than just trading baseball players. Longtime Dodgers executive Bob Graziano and FOX Television CEO Chase Carey were interested in buying SportsChannel Florida, which aired the Marlins' games, and one thing led to another and now Piazza was, as he said to his now-former teammates, ". . . with the Fishes."

He wouldn't be with the Fishes for long, though, and most conjecture had Piazza landing with his hometown Phillies, the Chicago Cubs, or even the Yankees, who were in the midst of a 114-win season but could upgrade at catcher, where they were platooning veteran Joe Girardi with unproven 26-year-old Jorge Posada.

Seven days after the trade—and after five games with the Marlins—Piazza and his agents believed the Cubs were closing in on a deal, But around noontime on May 22, a surprise suitor emerged: New York's National League team.

The Mets snapped a streak of six straight losing campaigns in 1997 by going 88–74 and remaining in the wild card race until the final week of the season. But they were scuffling in 1998 and in desperate need of some star power, especially with the Yankees enjoying a historic season across town. While Piazza was enduring his one week in Miami, the Mets were in the midst of a homestand in which they drew just 42,158 fans combined during three games against the Cincinnati Reds. Shea Stadium's maximum capacity: 57,333.

"We were trying to win back fans that had gone through some tough years with us," then-Mets general manager Steve Phillips said during an interview in 2016. "I remember [coowner] Mr. [Nelson] Doubleday calling me into a suite and looking over the stadium during a game and saying, 'Listen, we've got a good little team, but we need a superstar to get the fans hooked in.'"

Doubleday and fellow coowner Fred Wilpon were barely civil to each other, and it was no surprise they disagreed on the need to pursue

Piazza. Wilpon called into local sports talk radio show "Mike and the Mad Dog" to declare the Mets didn't need Piazza, after which Doubleday called in to say, oh yes, we do.

In 2016, Phillips said the Mets' baseball operations department was unanimous in trying to trade for Piazza and that Wilpon was serving as the voice of caution, asking whether or not it was worth the risk to send several prospects to the Marlins in exchange for an impending free agent when the team had already acquired impending free agents Al Leiter and Dennis Cook from Florida the previous winter.

By midafternoon May 22, the deal was done: Piazza for minor leaguers Geoff Goetz, Preston Wilson, and Ed Yarnall.

"That was one of the most remarkable times to flip the city upside down," Phillips said in 2016. "The Yankees are winning 114 games, and it stole the spotlight and gave the Mets fans a superstar and a reason to brag about it to their Yankees fan [friends]."

In New York, Piazza would have a chance to become the Mets' more personable answer to Derek Jeter, the coolly corporate face of a dynasty. Piazza possessed down-to-earth sensibilities and a gift of gab not usually associated with superstars. He enjoyed talking American history more than baseball, and his favorite music was 1980s hard rock, a genre that was scoffed at in real time before it was buried by grunge. The night before he was traded from the Dodgers, he spent time playing drums in a bar with a heavy metal cover band.

He also had an uncommon sense of self-awareness about the vagaries of fame.

"Sometimes I look around, and I think, 'What the hell am I doing here?'" Piazza told *Sports Illustrated* in 1993. "Someday someone is going to drag me away and put me in a Looney Tune."

A little more than seven years later, he'd find out just how prescient he was.

***

Piazza beat Clemens to New York by eight months, and in the aforementioned alternate timeline, perhaps the catcher could have prepared the pitcher for the cauldron he would enter and the immediate impatience of Big Apple sports fans. The Mets saw an immediate surge at the gate with Piazza, who went 1-for-4 with an RBI double in his debut May 23 in front of 32,908 fans.

But those fans expected perfection from their Hollywood import, who hit only .208 with runners in scoring position in his first nine weeks with the team and heard boos every time he didn't come through in the clutch. By early August, Piazza was miserable and withdrawn and potentially casting one eye toward the door.

"[Piazza] basically told me to have fun without him next year," one teammate told Bob Klapisch of the *Bergen Record*.

But Piazza finished the season with a flourish, batting .361 with 14 homers, 52 RBIs, and 32 extra-base hits in 183 at-bats over his final 53 games for the Mets, who missed the playoffs by a game. His performance down the stretch won over Mets fans and warmed Piazza to the idea of remaining in New York.

Piazza's agents and Phillips discussed a deal throughout the World Series, and the two sides agreed to a seven-year contract worth $91 million—less than Piazza wanted from the Dodgers, but still the richest contract in baseball history—on October 26 before Piazza could officially reach free agency.

Piazza said a couple calm months in New York convinced him the Big Apple was the place for him to establish some roots after the most chaotic season of his life.

"Why start over?" Piazza said. "What's the sense of filing and seeing what's out there? To me, I really believe I should be here."

Piazza had a lot going on in 1998, but at least he never had to worry about winning over new teammates with whom he'd nearly brawled mere months earlier. In his final start against the Yankees as a member of the Blue Jays on September 11, 1998, Clemens squandered a three-run lead in the fourth inning before plunking Scott Brosius in the back.

It wasn't the first time Clemens threw at or near a Yankees star. In his previous start against the Yankees on July 16, Clemens hit Jeter with a pitch.

Brosius exchanged words with Clemens as he walked to first base. Several members of the Yankees—not even four months removed from their fierce brawl with the Baltimore Orioles after Armando Benitez hit Tino Martinez in the back—barked at Clemens from the dugout.

Joe Torre argued Clemens should be ejected, but he got ejected himself while Clemens remained in the game.

"I said yesterday, Roger Clemens gets away with things that get other people thrown out of games," Torre said afterward. "This is a perfect example of that."

Clemens blamed a sore right hand, which he'd bruised while trying to field a pair of comebackers in the third inning, for his suddenly spotty command.

"It is strange that after we tied the score, his control got bad," Torre said.

In the top of the fifth inning, Hideki Irabu retaliated by hitting Blue Jays outfielder Shannon Stewart. Irabu then charged Stewart as both benches emptied for a fracas that resulted in five ejections. Darryl Strawberry, who threw a punch at somebody, ran to the Blue Jays dugout and dared Clemens to come onto the field. He remained seated.

One hundred and sixty days later, the enemy became a teammate. And on February 27, as Clemens prepared for his first batting practice session, Jeter and Chuck Knoblauch—whom Clemens used to throw at when the Red Sox and Minnesota Twins shared a spring training facility in Florida—came up with a way to welcome Clemens while also reminding him of their shared past.

Knoblauch, the Yankees' leadoff hitter, stepped into the batter's box covered from head to toe with catcher's equipment. Clemens, possessing his teeth-grinding intensity even during the first batting practice of the season, didn't initially notice Knoblauch's getup. Once he realized what was going on, Clemens grinned—and then threw a pitch behind Knoblauch.

"We have been ready for this one," Knoblauch told reporters.

Jeter then stepped to the plate wearing catcher's equipment plus an elbow guard and stood there as Clemens threw behind him.

"I didn't think I would get off that easy, but they better be careful because sometimes I don't miss," Clemens said with a smile that seemed to indicate he might not have been joking.

Such exchanges were rare between Clemens and the press covering the Yankees. While the freshly signed Piazza reported to Mets spring training in Port St. Lucie displaying a far more relaxed and engaging personality, Clemens had never been one for small talk.

Like all starting pitchers, Clemens was unapproachable the day of his starts. But his focus before taking the mound was more singular than anyone else's. While getting ready for a start with the Red Sox early in his career, Clemens once had no idea he'd knocked over an elderly reporter in the visiting clubhouse at Oakland Coliseum.

"I could walk right by my mother, and she'd be yelling in my ear, and I wouldn't even notice," Clemens once said of his prestart focus. "I've got my mind on something else."

Unlike most starting pitchers, Clemens extended his no-interview policy to the day before his starts. And while there was no official declaration by Clemens that he wouldn't talk on the other days, he was also rarely visible during the period writers had access to the locker room.

Writers weren't the only ones who barely saw Clemens outside of his starts. In 2000, Klapisch wrote Clemens ". . . remains a mystery to virtually everyone in the clubhouse, not to mention Joe Torre and the coaching staff" and noted his absence in an otherwise tight-knit locker room filled with players who enjoyed poring over each game, win or lose.

Added Klapisch: "Clemens hardly ever socializes with the Yankees, either at home or on the road. He's rarely at his locker, killing time with

Jeter or O'Neill or Martinez, choosing instead to pour himself into his between-starts exercise regimen."

Yankees fans, of course, didn't care how sociable a guy was as long as he performed. But Clemens's singular focus didn't translate to the mound in 1999, when he posted a career-high 4.60 ERA and threw just 187 ⅔ innings—his fewest in a nonstrike season since 1985—while missing time with a left hamstring injury.

Despite the subpar numbers, Clemens still earned the win in his first five decisions, which gave him an American League-record 20 straight victorious decisions dating back to June 3, 1998. But a pair of streaks ended against the Mets on June 6, when Clemens gave up seven runs over 2 ⅔ innings—the earliest he'd departed for performance reasons since July 1995—and took the loss as the Yankees fell, 7–2.

The biggest culprit against Clemens at Yankee Stadium that night? Mike Piazza, who doubled to lead off a four-run second inning and hit a two-run homer in a three-run third.

It was the second straight time Piazza experienced success against Clemens. The two faced off for the first time in an interleague game on June 30, 1998, when Piazza went 2-for-4 with a pair of singles against Clemens, who threw a 141-pitch complete game in the Blue Jays' 6–3 victory.

"I remember thinking, hmm, I see the ball pretty well off this dude," Piazza wrote in his autobiography.

Clemens never got nearly that comfortable in his first season in pinstripes. While the Yankees cruised to another AL East title, fans began losing patience with the luxury item they didn't need to win the World Series in historic fashion the previous season. Finally, on July 15—two days shy of the one-year anniversary of his beaning of Jeter—Clemens was booed off the mound at Yankee Stadium after he gave up six runs over six innings and took the loss to the Braves.

Prior to this next start, Clemens changed his uniform number from 12 to 22. But that didn't do much to alter his fortunes: he went 6–6 with a 4.23 ERA over his final 14 regular-season starts.

Clemens opened the playoffs with an impressive effort by tossing seven scoreless innings of three-hit ball and earning the win as the Yankees eliminated the Rangers in Game Three of the AL Division Series. But his next start, in Game Three of the AL Championship Series against the Red Sox, would further cement his reputation as someone who failed to produce in the playoffs.

Pitching in Boston against Pedro Martinez—the pitcher who replaced Clemens as the Red Sox staff ace and resident icon—Clemens was booed as he warmed up. The Fenway Park crowd got what it wanted to see as the Red Sox lit up Clemens for five runs in two-plus innings on their way to a 13–1 win—the biggest margin of victory ever in an ALCS game.

Clemens's playoff ERA rose to 4.04. By the late innings, Red Sox fans were chanting, "Where is Rog-er? In the show-er!"

"It was such an adrenaline rush hearing our fans," Red Sox outfielder Darren Lewis told the *Los Angeles Times*. "They were so loud and enthusiastic, it was like you were on a natural high out there. We loved it."

The loss was the only one the Yankees would absorb in the playoffs. For the World Series, Clemens was slotted to the back of the rotation. By the time he took the mound for Game Four against the Atlanta Braves, the Yankees' 25th world championship was a sure thing, and his solid performance—one run over 7 ⅓ innings in a 4-1 victory—as the winning pitcher did nothing to improve his spotty postseason reputation.

Clemens was reminded of this when the Yankees received their World Series rings. Each player's name was inscribed along with his number. Except Clemens's number "mistakenly" read 33—the number worn with the Yankees by David Wells, the profane but beloved pitcher George Steinbrenner had to be convinced to include in the Clemens trade. Nobody, least of all Clemens, believed the mistake was actually a mistake.

Unfortunately for Clemens, he didn't do much in the first half of

2000 to distance himself from his predecessor in the Yankees' rotation. While he struck out 13 in a memorable complete-game loss to Martinez and the Red Sox on May 28, Clemens gave up five runs or more seven times in his first 13 starts. He once again bottomed out against Piazza and the Mets, this time on June 9, when Piazza hit a grand slam in the third inning of the Mets' 12–2 win.

In his next start, Clemens lasted just an inning before exiting due to a groin injury that required a trip to the disabled list. In 44 starts for the Yankees, Clemens had a 4.65 ERA. He was about to turn 38 and offering no evidence at all he was about to return to his former glory.

But he was close to resuming his role as baseball's most polarizing pitcher.

***

Clemens returned from the disabled list July 2 and earned the win by limiting the Tampa Bay Devil Rays to one run over seven innings. His next start lined up six days later for what promised to be a memorable day and night in New York baseball history—the first two-stadium doubleheader between Big Apple teams in almost a century.

Due to a rainout of a scheduled game at Yankee Stadium in June, the Yankees and Mets were going to play the middle game of a three-game series at Shea Stadium in the afternoon before playing the makeup game at Yankee Stadium around 7 p.m. It was the first split doubleheader in New York since September 7, 1903, when the Brooklyn Superbas (the predecessors to the Dodgers) and New York Giants played a game apiece at their home stadia.

Anticipating sellout crowds in both 55,000-plus seat parks, the New York City Transit Authority added seven trains to the No. 7, No. 4, and D lines. Travel was going to be far easier for the teams: the path between Shea Stadium and Yankee Stadium was closed for the team buses, allowing for a 15-minute ride along the Grand Central Parkway, over the Triborough Bridge, and onto the Major Deegan Expressway.

"It kind of took you back to high school, where you play one game, you jump on a bus, you drive across town, you play another game," Yankees outfielder Paul O'Neill says.

Steinbrenner recognized the doubleheader as not only a chance to hand the Mets two losses, but an opportunity to tweak them. While Clemens was lined up for the nightcap, the Yankees needed a spot starter for the first game and recalled from the minor leagues Dwight Gooden, the one-time Mets ace whose career had been derailed by drug issues before he signed with the Yankees in 1996 and threw a no-hitter before going on to win a total of 11 games and a World Series ring.

Gooden, thirty-five years old, appeared done when his hometown Devil Rays released him after he posted a 6.63 ERA in eight starts. But Steinbrenner called again and asked Gooden if he'd like to report to the Yankees' spring training facility, also located in Tampa. Gooden went to work with organizational pitching coordinator Billy Connors and made two starts with the Yankees' rookie-level Gulf Coast League affiliate, for whom he allowed four hits over eight scoreless innings.

"And then Mr. Steinbrenner called me into his office," Gooden told the *New York Post* in 2016. "I thought he was going to release me. He said, 'We need a pitcher in New York against the Mets. Are you ready?' I said yes. I probably wasn't ready, but I wanted to go to Shea one more time."

Gooden had not pitched at Shea Stadium since his final game with the Mets on June 24, 1994.

"It's an event within an event," Mets manager Bobby Valentine said. "It'll be interesting to see how it turns out."

Valentine had no idea how right he'd be, but for reasons that had nothing to do with Gooden.

The day got off to an odd start with the first pitch of the game from the Mets' Bobby Jones. Chuck Knoblauch hit a liner to right-center field but was thrown out trying to extend the single into a double.

As Knoblauch jogged off the field, Yankees first base coach—and former Mets all-star—Lee Mazzilli argued that Knoblauch had been interfered with by first baseman Todd Zeile. While the two players didn't brush up against each other, Mazzilli said Zeile was in the basepath and Knoblauch had to change his path to avoid Zeile. First base umpire Rob Cook, a Triple-A umpire serving as a fill-in, agreed with Mazzilli and awarded Knoblauch second base. Valentine argued to no avail and was ejected.

Derek Jeter followed with an RBI single, and the Yankees never trailed in a 4–2 victory. Gooden earned the win by allowing two runs in five innings. It would be his final appearance at Shea Stadium.

After the game, players on both teams boarded their buses and were generally enthusiastic about the history they were about to make.

"I do remember feeling just as energized and ready to play for the nightcap," Zeile says. "It didn't feel like we'd already played a game."

A notable exception, in more ways than one, was Piazza, who was batting .348 and in the midst of his best season with the Mets. Since he lived in New Jersey, Piazza wanted to have his car with him for an easier trip home, so he drove from Shea Stadium to Yankee Stadium. And as he did, he kept feeling as if something were amiss, writing in his autobiography that ". . . the entire day had a weird-energy, full-moon vibe to it."

Piazza's uneasy feeling was amplified when Clemens buzzed leadoff hitter Lenny Harris. After taking Clemens's first pitch in the second inning, Piazza—now 7-for-12 with three homers against Clemens—had an ". . . inexplicable premonition," as he explained in his book, that something sinister was about to happen.

Clemens's next pitch, a two-seam fastball, sailed up and in on Piazza. At the last possible instant, Piazza ducked while pulling his arms close to his head. The ball hit Piazza in the helmet and he fell to the ground, barely conscious, staring and blinking blankly at the sky.

With the assistance of Valentine and trainer Fred Hina, Piazza got up and slowly walked off the field. A Yankees doctor was waiting to evaluate him when he got to the visiting clubhouse, but first, there was someone on the phone.

Clemens, more than 15 years removed from writing a letter to Detroit Tigers farmhand Ronald Davis insisting he meant to hit him in the knee and not to send him to the hospital with a concussion, was on the other line.

Per his autobiography, Piazza took the phone and threw it. "Tell him to go fuck himself," he said.

Piazza was taken to a local hospital where, like Davis, he was diagnosed with a concussion—no small ailment, but far better than what could have been the alternative. He wrote he believed that if he hadn't ducked, the fastball from Clemens ". . . would have struck me in the eye and possibly killed me."

Piazza returned home, where he found some humor in the situation.

"Want to hear something really funny?" Piazza said the next day. "When I got home last night after getting beaned, I have an acoustic guitar that Garth Brooks gave me from spring training. And I went over and played it.

"You ever hear that story where people get hit in the head and something happens, and next thing you know, they have this weird ability that they never had? Nah, I still can't play guitar."

Piazza was able to laugh about his lack of musical skills postbeaning, but he was in no mood to smile about what happened as he met the media during a press conference prior to the Mets-Yankees finale on July 10. Piazza said he had no interest in fielding a phone call from Clemens and joined Valentine in declaring he believed Clemens threw at him on purpose.

"I don't want to say he intentionally hit me in the head, but I think he intentionally threw at my head," Piazza said.

"We handed his lunch to him, so he threw at the first guy, threw at the second guy, and hit the third guy," Valentine said.

Piazza was asked if he thought Clemens's actions were cowardly.

"You know what?" Piazza said. "I do."

Clemens didn't speak on the record that Sunday, but Klapisch was among a group of reporters who told him of Piazza's response to the cowardice question. Wrote Klapisch:

"Roger Clemens' shoulders sunk ever so slightly, his eyes flickering downward, revealing just how stunned he was. Why? Everyone in the baseball community already knew the answer, but for the first time since he assaulted Mike Piazza with a 95-mph fastball, Clemens was hearing first-hand that he was a coward.

*Coward.*"

The Mets were even angrier behind closed doors than they were at the podium. They were furious with Clemens, of course, who had spent his entire career in the American League, where he could intimidate batters with high and hard fastballs without ever having to worry about stepping into a batter's box himself.

With one notable exception, the Mets had unusual allies in the Yankees locker room. Yankees players, barely two years removed from their galvanizing brawl with the Baltimore Orioles and even more recently on the receiving end of Clemens's purpose pitches, understood the fury of their rivals.

"One hundred percent understood both sides of the issue," says Yankees third baseman Scott Brosius, who was hit by Clemens in 1998. "We'd been on the other side of it. Roger's competitive, and he didn't like to get beat, and he's going to do everything in his power to win. So throwing inside is part of the deal. And then hitting guys is part of the deal.

"I was pissed off when he hit me. That's how it works."

Tino Martinez, who had been hit in the middle of the back by the Armando Benitez pitch that started the 1998 fight between the Yankees and Orioles, walked to first base without hesitation when Glendon Rusch plunked him on the backside the bottom of the second inning the night earlier.

"Basically, it was payback for Piazza getting hit," Martinez told the *New York Post* in 2016. "I wasn't going to do anything. I didn't want to make a scene. Basically, the Mets had to hit somebody. It's part of the game."

The Mets' harshest fury was reserved for Yankees manager Joe Torre, who had been a vocal critic of Clemens during the exchange of beanballs between the Yankees and Clemens's Blue Jays in 1998. Two years later, he was the only member of the Yankees speaking in defense of Clemens, and to the Mets, his words sounded flimsy and hypocritical.

"Roger knows what it takes for a pitcher to be successful, and that's to throw inside," Torre said. "His fastball's not straight. It's got a lot of movement and a lot of explosion. I think that had a lot to do with what happened."

An uncomfortable buzz filled Shea Stadium in the hours before Mike Hampton took the mound for the Mets as players, fans, and writers alike wondered if the Mets would try and exact revenge for Piazza. Would Chuck Knoblauch, Derek Jeter, or Bernie Williams wear a high, hard one?

Would a full-fledged brawl break out on the field . . . or before the teams ever reached the diamond? Mets General Manager Steve Phillips took the unusual step of closing off the weight room, which was normally shared by the home and visiting teams and which was accessible only via the Mets locker room.

"I was like, wow, this is a different level kind of stuff," Yankees pitcher David Cone says.

"That's really not a big deal," Martinez told the *New York Post* in 2016. "It was almost the smart thing to do. If Roger wanted a workout, and Piazza's around there, if anything else escalates . . ."

As detailed the next morning by Klapisch, Valentine, who had been seriously injured by a beanball as a minor leaguer, told Hampton and the rest of the Mets pitchers there would be no retaliation. Hampton tossed seven scoreless innings, and Benitez closed out a 2–0 win that ensured the Mets would not be swept in the four-game, three-day, two-stadium, one-memorable-issue series.

There were no more regular-season games scheduled between the intracity rivals. And at his press conference prior to the Mets' series-ending win, Piazza expressed his hope that the issue would soon fade away.

"I want to say I will address this issue for the first and last time," Piazza said.

Not quite.

***

The question on everyone's mind from the moment the Yankees clinched the pennant: when would Clemens pitch against the Mets?

From July 2—the start before he beaned Piazza—through the end of the season, Clemens looked more like the Clemens of old by going 9–2 with a 3.00 ERA in 18 starts. The strong finish lowered Clemens's ERA to 3.70, the second-lowest mark in the AL behind only Pedro Martinez's superhuman 1.74 mark.

Clemens opened the playoffs by losing his two starts in the AL Division Series against the Oakland Athletics. He was slotted in as the Yankees' fourth starter for the AL Championship Series against the Mariners and responded with the best postseason start of his career—eight one-hit innings in which Clemens struck out 17 as the Yankees took a three-games-to-one lead with a 5–0 win.

He also threw up and in at Mariners superstar shortstop Alex Rodriguez, which angered Seattle manager Lou Piniella.

"He has made a pretty good reputation for himself doing that," Piniella told the *San Francisco Chronicle*.

Even with the dominant outing against the Mariners, Clemens was arguably the Yankees' third-best option for a big playoff game behind Andy Pettitte and Orlando "El Duque" Hernandez. But once the Yankees eliminated the Mariners in six games, Torre elected to start Pettitte and Clemens, with his reasoning that they were the next two in line to follow after Game Six.

"This was Andy's turn, and Roger falls in behind Andy," Torre said prior to Game Two of the World Series. "If we had to play Game Seven against Seattle, Roger would have pitched this first game. So I just didn't do anything, because, really, it's tough to pick and choose with El Duque, Roger, and Andy as far as who I'd rather pitch such-and-such."

Of course, it also meant Clemens would pitch at home, where the designated hitter was utilized, and not at Shea Stadium, where he was 0–2 with a 5.79 ERA in four career starts, including Game Six of the 1986 World Series.

Clemens and Piazza both tried dismissing their shared history in the days leading up to the World Series.

"Let's just say that, to me, it's definitely something in the past," Piazza told *Newsday*. "I can't go up there and even think about it. I've still got to hit. It's in the past. I don't see it as a big rematch, something to be settled between us, whether he gets me out or I get a hit."

Clemens attempted to diffuse the situation as well and admitted he felt bad about hitting Piazza. But as he was prone to doing in Boston, the more Clemens talked, the more bizarre he sounded—this time by suggesting Piazza got hit in the head because he threw up his arms to avoid the ball.

"I think it hit part of his hand and ricocheted to his head," Clemens said. "You just don't want to be in that area. Any time you are, it's a mistake."

According to *Newsday*, Piazza laughed for 15 seconds when informed of Clemens's comments before peppering his response with the type of pop culture and historical references he'd become known for.

"So they're all claiming I'm a proverbial David Copperfield of baseball, the old sleight-of-hand?" Piazza told the newspaper. "That's pretty good. It's like the movie *JFK*. It's just like the whole commission, an entire cover-up. That's pretty funny, dude. You could do stand-up with this stuff."

Piazza lamented the possibility his first at-bat against Clemens would overshadow the World Series.

"It's like the only thing [people are] talking about," Piazza said. "They're not talking about Pettitte versus Leiter. They're not talking about the World Series. Everyone is waiting for that first pitch he throws me.

"It might be the most-watched pitch in history. Millions of eyeballs will be glued to the TV."

Piazza might have been the only one feeling something amiss in the universe the afternoon and early evening of July 9. But as the first pitch of Game 2 approached, players on both sides sensed an uneasy buzz.

"There was some testosterone in the air that night," Mets backup catcher Todd Pratt says.

Clemens—surely aware of his reputation as a shaky playoff pitcher and the unanimity with which he was regarded as the bad guy in his rivalry with Piazza—was intense, even by his standards, in the hours before he took the mound. As part of his pregame routine, Clemens had a trainer apply hot ointment to his . . . well, his private parts.

"Clemens was like a middle linebacker in the SEC—he was frothing at the mouth before he wanted to pitch," Yankees pitcher David Cone says. "He had hot stuff all over his body. He had a mouthpiece like a linebacker. That was his mentality. Almost couldn't even look at him, much less talk to him. He was so fired up in his own little zone. I had never seen anyone to that extreme."

Clemens's intensity was apparent even on television. After pumping 97 mph fastballs in striking out leadoff batter Timo Perez, Clemens licked his lips, grimaced, shook his head, and glared during an at-bat against Edgardo Alfonzo in which he hit 98 mph on the radar gun and struck out the second baseman.

Up to the plate stepped Piazza, and the at-bat everyone had waited to see for 104 days was finally here. With flashbulbs popping throughout the stadium, Piazza, as was his custom, watched the first pitch, a fastball on the inside corner for a called strike. He also took a called strike two, another inside fastball, before Clemens's third pitch, a split-fingered fastball, sailed low and outside for ball one.

In the broadcast booth, Joe Buck reminded viewers of the one-sided nature of the pitcher-batter rivalry.

"Piazza 7 out of 12 in his career against Clemens with three home runs, nine RBIs."

Clemens's fourth pitch was a fastball that bore in on Piazza, who swung and made contact but broke his bat while doing so. The ball bounced into foul territory, its path followed by the FOX cameras. The ball skipped into the Yankees dugout, where someone in a Yankees jacket went to retrieve it as the crowd roared and America began to learn what was happening off-camera courtesy of a bemused-sounding Buck.

"The barrel of the bat comes back at Roger Clemens and he fires the bat back toward Piazza, who was going down the first base line," Buck said.

In the moment after Piazza made contact, Clemens appeared to go into a fielding position, which backed up his eventual contention he thought it was the ball. Piazza, unaware of where the ball landed, began running toward first base and looked upward.

"To that point, I think Roger thought he might have gotten Mike out and jammed him," Mets first baseman Todd Zeile says. "I think Mike wasn't quite sure where the ball was.

"And then the bat's being thrown at him."

The bat skipped toward Clemens, who did sort of an awkward jig before he made a juggling catch. And then, with his gaze apparently fixed on Piazza, he fired the bat toward the first base line.

"Roger's just wired for the game, and this thing comes at him," Scott Brosius says. "He's not even in his right mind when he throws it. It's just 'Get out of here.'"

"He went and he grabbed it, and I just think it was adrenaline, 'Get this thing out of here,'" former Yankees media relations director Rick Cerrone says.

By the time the cameras whirled back to the field, the benches were emptying and nobody could quite believe what was happening.

"That was surreal, sitting out in the bullpen, watching from afar," Cone says.

"My first reaction is, 'Oh crap, are you kidding me?'" Brosius says.

"I thought there was going to be a fight," Jose Vizcaino says.

"I'm like, how could this be, on this stage, at this time, in this moment to have that happen?" Zeile says. "It's crazy."

"The two stars, given the history between the two—I think, to be honest, the umpires were in shock, didn't know what to do," Pratt says.

Piazza was slowing down as he realized the ball went foul, but as the remains of his bat sailed by him, he took another couple steps up the first base line. Then he turned, flipped what was left of his bat over so that he was holding the jagged edge in his palm, and started walking toward Clemens.

"You see something coming at you, you get down to field it, you recognize it's the bat and he's just kind of like, 'Get this out of here,'" Zeile says. "And it might happen to be Mike being on the line. I think only after that happened did they kind of square up and look at each other like, 'Oh, this is an incident now.'"

As Piazza made his way toward the mound and the benches emptied, Clemens yelled, "I thought it was the ball," and patted his chest. Home plate umpire Charlie Reliford and Yankees catcher Jorge Posada stepped in between Clemens and Piazza before Mets bench coach John Stearns raced in to further pull Piazza away from Clemens.

It took less than a minute for Piazza to hit the most famous foul ball in history, for the benches to empty, and for players and coaches to return to their dugouts, bullpens, and positions without a single punch being thrown. But that was enough time for FOX broadcasters Buck, Tim McCarver, and Bob Brenly to try and begin deciphering what they'd just seen.

"That is all Roger Clemens there," Buck said as the teams were still gathered near the pitcher's mound. "A moment started by—created by—Clemens, and thankfully not much more on the field than these two benches emptying and the players [pause] now in a moment of standing around and trying to sort out what just happened. That was surprising."

"Joe, there were a lot of people who defended Roger Clemens when he hit Mike Piazza in the head—I was one of them," McCarver said. "In my view, right now, Roger Clemens is dead wrong. You can't take up the better part of the bat, the fat part of the bat, and fire it into foul territory near Piazza."

As McCarver began uttering his third sentence, a replay aired—the first of many thousands of replays.

A second replay aired as McCarver paused.

"Man, that is . . . I'll tell you, that is a blatant act right there. Piazza has every right to be upset. Wow."

After McCarver spoke, FOX displayed a split screen, with Clemens on the left throwing a baseball into his mitt and appearing to decline an offer of a warm-up and Piazza on the right walking to the plate with a new bat.

Buck explained as a third replay aired that Clemens basically had thrown a jagged piece of wood that ended up about two feet away from Mike Piazza.

As Brenly acknowledged, fortunately Piazza was looking at Clemens when he threw the bat, or he might have run right into its barrel.

Moments later, Clemens delivered his next pitch. Piazza checked his swing and rolled a grounder to the right side. Jose Vizcaino fielded it cleanly and threw out a hard-charging Piazza.

"And a perfect first inning for Clemens," Buck said, as Clemens walked off the mound, patted his chest, and said, "My fault," while talking to Reliford. Piazza turned back to the field twice, each time offering what appeared to be a bemused-looking glare, before donning his catcher's gear and heading out for the bottom of the inning.

After his talk with Reliford, Clemens marched into the dugout, disappeared into a slightly sloped tunnel, and walked uphill toward the Yankees locker room.

"Roger, after the inning was over, went into my office—where, by the way, Mel Stottlemyre had come out of the hospital to watch the game with George in my office," Torre says, referring to the beloved

Yankees pitching coach who was battling multiple myeloma and could not be among crowds.

Torre, Stottlemyre, and Steinbrenner were about to see an unusually—and immediately—contrite Clemens.

"He went up there and he was crying because of what transpired," Torre says. "He just realized what he almost did."

The Yankees did their best to give Clemens some time to calm down and collect his thoughts during a long bottom of the first in which they scored twice—via RBI singles by Tino Martinez and Posada—and forced Mets starter Mike Hampton to throw 32 pitches.

That was more than enough cushion for Clemens, who emerged from Torre's office and was almost as dominant as he'd been eight days earlier against the Mariners. He allowed just two hits—both singles to Zeile—walked none, and struck out nine while facing just four batters over the minimum in eight scoreless innings.

The performance was notable for reasons beyond what happened in the first inning. Clemens entered Game Two with a 6.65 ERA in eight career starts against the Mets. He'd been particularly ineffective since joining the Yankees: in four interleague starts, Clemens allowed 22 runs over 21 innings.

The Yankees, meanwhile, added individual runs in the second, fifth, seventh, and eighth innings while putting a runner on in every inning except the fourth. They also took advantage of three errors by the Mets, who made the miscues within the first three innings.

Given Clemens's unusual dominance and the Mets' atypically messy play—the three errors were one fewer than they committed in the first 10 playoff games—one had to wonder whether the Mets were intimidated by Clemens's behavior in the first inning.

"I don't know how much that had to do with it, guys and gals," Mets manager Bobby Valentine said afterward. "I have no idea about that stuff."

Or were the Mets distracted over whether or not they should have fought Clemens and the Yankees? In the regular season, there was little doubt a brawl would have broken out. But on the biggest stage of all?

"I was a little surprised Piazza didn't go out there and start a brawl—it was that egregious for me," Brenly says. "But I guess given the circumstances and the stage, that's probably the last thing anybody wanted, a brawl in the middle of the field, especially with a stadium full of Yankees and Mets fans.

"But I definitely think Clemens was in the wrong, and I definitely think if that would have been a regular-season [game], they might still be out there rolling around on the grass."

"People say that if it was [the] regular season, it might have been a different story," Vizcaino says.

Still, there was clearly some disagreement within the Mets' locker room over how Piazza should have handled the situation. Piazza hinted after the game he would have gone after Clemens if the pitcher had looked at him or said something profane. Friends of Piazza confirmed as much the next day. But Clemens kept declaring he thought it was the ball and kept asking for a new ball to resume the game.

"I said, 'What is your problem?'" Piazza said following the game. "I kept asking him, 'What is your problem?' He didn't say anything. If he would have said something, maybe it would have been a little different. I don't know."

Hampton, who took the loss after allowing four runs in six innings, generated headlines when he questioned why Piazza didn't fight Clemens. Hampton was also the pitcher on July 9, when he followed Valentine's orders and didn't seek retaliation the night after Clemens beaned Piazza.

"I think we should've fought, to be honest with you," Hampton said. "But that's not my call. You can't make something happen if guys aren't going to defend themselves. Different people react differently. Mike's a little calmer. I'm more hot-tempered. I would've reacted a little differently."

Pratt, one of the Mets' emotional leaders, says the "to fight or not to fight" debate still crops up regularly.

"I get asked that question all the time: 'Would you have reacted different?'" Pratt says. "Thinking about it, I think it all went down the right way—no fight. It's the most important games; we couldn't. Everybody else wants to fight; we probably wanted to fight at that point. But you look at that game, and we need to win."

Mets reliever Turk Wendell didn't think there should have been a fight. But he was outspoken the next day, when he declared anyone else pitching at any other time of the year would have been thrown out of the game. His feelings didn't soften over the next two decades.

"I just look back on that, and I just say gosh, if that was Jeter up to bat, and I did that, I would have been kicked out of the game in a heartbeat," Wendell says. "Roger's a great competitor. Obviously an unbelievable career. But for him to come out and say he thought it was the ball—well, I mean, we're not playing Little League or Wiffle ball, where you throw the ball at the guy and he's out.

"He throws the bat—what if he struck Mike with it? I mean, holy cow. Then benches would have really cleared."

Or maybe the simplest explanation would suffice on a night with few answers to the questions on everyone's minds: maybe Clemens just had a second straight terrific performance in the postseason.

"Roger was really good that night," Zeile says. "He was able to work through Mike, who had been a guy that really had dominated him. And so we just never really got anything going. I mean, obviously, I had the only two hits and those were spread out.

"You've kind of got to tip your hat to the job that he did. He was good that night."

The Mets tried to generate a second storyline in the ninth inning, when they scored five runs against the normally reliable duo of Jeff Nelson and Mariano Rivera. Left fielder Clay Bellinger robbed Zeile of a three-run homer against Rivera, who gave up a two-out, two-run homer down the right field line to Jay Payton before striking out Kurt Abbott to lock up the victory.

But afterward, nobody cared about how close the Mets came to evening the game or the series. Nobody really even cared about Clemens's dominance. It was all about the bat.

"Even Roger after the game, he was like, 'Are you kidding me? It had to be Piazza,'" Brosius says. "Because really, the last thing he wanted was to keep stirring that up. It had just been so overplayed and so overtalked about."

Clemens, who would eventually be fined $50,000 for throwing the bat, was more composed at his postgame press conference than he might have been during his peak years with the Red Sox. He reminded reporters he'd tried calling Piazza after hitting the catcher in the head in July. Clemens declared six times there was no intent behind his bat toss and acknowledged he was, as some teammates later put it, not quite in his right mind when he threw the bat.

"My emotions, I'm telling you, my feet were off the ground," Clemens said.

And why was that?

"It's not too hard to figure it out," Clemens said.

Neither Joe Torre nor Rick Cerrone, the Yankees' director of media relations, said anything as they walked from Torre's office to the cramped press conference room in the bowels of Yankee Stadium.

"He knew that was going to be the takeaway from the win," Cerrone says. "We won the game, but we know that was what they were going to talk about."

Torre's accessibility, calm demeanor, New York background, and three World Series rings had earned him almost unprecedented rope from a large and inquisitive press corps. But as he and Cerrone anticipated, Torre was on the defensive from the moment he took his seat.

"I think we have to ask one other question: why would he throw it at him?" Torre said. "So he could get thrown out of the game in the second game of the World Series? Does that make any sense to anybody? Somebody answer me. You guys ask me questions. Somebody answer my questions. Why would he do it?"

At one point, Torre got up from the podium and stormed out of the room. He eventually returned, though he was only marginally less angry.

"I was so upset because, guys, it's the World Series," Torre says. "He's not going to do something to jeopardize his being able to pitch in the World Series. It just didn't make sense, you know?"

At the very least, the two rivals, now engaged in a fiercer battle than ever before, found common ground in finding it difficult, then and now, to understand just what had transpired between two of the game's biggest superstars.

"You go back and watch the video, you're still watching it [and] you don't believe it that that happened," Vizcaino says. "It was just crazy. And not only that, but then he was able to set up and threw eight great innings.

"And it was just like, wow, it's crazy the way it started. But it was even better the way it finished."

# CHAPTER 3
# GAME THREE

**Mets 4, Yankees 2**
**Yankees lead series, two games to one**

**IN 1963, RON** Hunt was a 22-year-old on his way to a second-place finish in the Rookie of the Year balloting and a solid career in which he'd make the All-Star team twice. He'd also been hit by a pitch 243 times, the most in the modern era at the time of his retirement.

But neither what he was accomplishing, nor the promise he held, was enough to overcome the stigma of the jersey he was wearing prior to a home game at the Polo Grounds.

"Met my first Met fan, come down the 20-some odd steps in center field," Hunt said in 2019. "About halfway down, I heard this little kid say, 'Hey, 33.' I looked up at a 12-year-old face. Said, 'What can I do for you?'

"He said, 'Whose reject are you?'"

Thirty-seven years later, the Mets were nobody's idea of rejects. But the 2000 National League pennant winners were an eclectic bunch filled with castoffs from other teams and star-caliber players who'd faced plenty of obstacles on their way to New York.

The team was assembled by an odd couple—a 37-year-old general manager who exuded corporate cool and a 50-year-old, candid-to-a-fault manager—who agreed on little but were united by scouting and developmental viewpoints shaped by the struggles they'd experienced as professional baseball players.

The 2000 Mets weren't rejects, but led by Steve Phillips and Bobby Valentine, they embodied a franchise that always welcomed and appealed to the easily dismissed, especially in a market dominated by the imperial Yankees. And in Game Three, the Mets and their fans got to enjoy one night in the World Series spotlight.

***

The Mets didn't play a game until April 11, 1962, but their debut was the end of a decades-long process executed by the most powerful man in post-World War II New York City.

As suburbia took root in the areas surrounding the five boroughs and the car was transformed from a luxury item into a necessity, Robert Moses, who was the Triborough Bridge and Tunnel Authority chairman, oversaw the construction of several highways and bridges that made the city easily accessible for a newly remote and mobile population.

Baseball in New York, though, remained decidedly friendly to those who relied on mass transit. The most beloved stadia of the first half of the 1900s, the Polo Grounds and Yankee Stadium, were near the heart of Manhattan and easily accessible via nearby subway stops. Ebbets Field was considered too distant and inconvenient because the Brooklyn destination was a long subway ride or expensive cab ride for Manhattan fans.

But with all three stadia beginning to show their age, Moses hatched a plan to build a stadium in Queens at Flushing Meadows—site of the 1934 World's Fair—and lure the Dodgers to play there. Moses envisioned a city-owned 50,000-plus-seat facility located at the intersection of multiple highways and equipped with acres of parking lots.

Moses's proposal was rejected by Dodgers owner Walter O'Malley, who wanted to move his team to a stadium located in downtown Brooklyn at the intersection of Atlantic Avenue and Flatbush Avenue, where fans could arrive via the subway and the Long Island Railroad. In addition, O'Malley had no interest in paying rent to New York City.

Plus, as he noted, the Brooklyn Dodgers wouldn't be the Brooklyn Dodgers if they were in Queens.

The standoff continued for the better part of a decade—until the 1957 season, when O'Malley asked Giants owner Horace Stoneham if he would join him in relocating to California. Despite winning the World Series in 1954 and the presence of Willie Mays in center field, the Giants drew just 650,000 fans to the rapidly aging Polo Grounds in 1956.

In May 1957, National League owners voted to allow both the Dodgers and Giants to move to California with the condition they do so following the season. Last-ditch negotiations continued but were unsuccessful, and in September, the Los Angeles City Council voted to give the Dodgers 307 acres at Chavez Ravine, where O'Malley would build a privately funded stadium.

Within five days in late September, the Dodgers and Giants each played their final home games in New York City. After half a century in which the Dodgers and Giants regularly battled for the right to face the Yankees in the World Series, New York was suddenly a one-team town.

Mayor Robert Wagner Jr. wasted little time in trying to replace the Dodgers and Giants. A committee headed by lawyer William A. Shea tried unsuccessfully to lure an existing franchise to New York. Then, when Major League Baseball refused to add teams via expansion, Shea teamed up with former Dodgers general manager Branch Rickey to form the Continental League, which would have franchises in New York as well as seven other cities lacking a Major League Baseball franchise.

Rickey announced in early 1960 that the Continental League would begin play in April 1961. Major League Baseball blinked and agreed to add four teams, including a National League entry in New York, over a two-year span—all in markets that would have been served by the Continental League. The announcement was made by no other than Walter O'Malley.

The Washington Senators and Los Angeles Angels began play in the American League in 1961, and the Mets and Houston Astros followed suit in the National League in 1962. The Continental League, having served its purpose, disbanded in August 1960.

While Moses engaged in bitter and fruitless negotiations with O'Malley regarding the proposed stadium at Flushing Meadows, he found a far more agreeable partner in Joan Payson, the owner of New York's new National League team. Payson and New York City came to terms on a 30-year lease in 1961 with the option to renew for another 10 years.

Payson decided on the name "Mets" in honor of the metropolitan area in which the team would play as well as an homage to the New York Metropolitans, who played in the American Association from 1883 through 1887.

The Mets' logo, hat, and colors would also pay tribute to the city the team would call home as well as to its predecessors in the National League. The logo pictured a bridge and a skyline representing buildings connected to each of the five boroughs. The Mets wore blue and orange uniforms, an acknowledgment of the official colors of New York State as well as an homage to the color schemes of the teams the Mets were replacing. And the NY atop their hats was embroidered in blue and orange.

The Mets were taking the spot of the Dodgers and Giants, but they were going to be most influenced by the men responsible for the

Yankees' recent dynastic run. George Weiss and Casey Stengel oversaw the most successful tenure in baseball history from 1949 through 1960, when, with Weiss as the general manager and Stengel serving as manager, the Yankees won 10 pennants and seven World Series, including a record five in a row from 1949 to 1953. Of the Yankees' seven titles, five were achieved with Subway Series triumphs over the Dodgers or Giants.

But after the Yankees fell to the Pirates in the 1960 World Series—a seven-game affair in which the former earned their three wins by at least 10 runs apiece—the Yankees did not offer Stengel a new contract. Co-owner Dan Topping said the Yankees were moving on from Stengel because they wanted to make sure manager-in-waiting Ralph Houk, who was the first base coach in 1960, wasn't hired by another team. Topping also said Stengel's age, 70, was a factor, to which Stengel later said, "I'll never make the mistake of being 70 again."

Weiss was also not retained by the Yankees, but it didn't take long for the men to partner up with New York's new National League team. Weiss was named the Mets' general manager in May 1961 and spent the next several months asking Stengel, who had gotten a job working at a bank owned by his wife's family, to join him. Finally, in October, Stengel agreed and returned to the dugout as the Mets' inaugural manager.

Stengel, who played for the Dodgers and Giants before his historic run as Yankees manager, would be making his Mets debut in a familiar spot. While Shea Stadium—named in honor of the lawyer who brought National League baseball back to New York—was being built, the Mets agreed to play one season at the Polo Grounds.

But one season at the Polo Grounds turned into two. For better and for worse, the 2,002,638 fans who turned out in those two years saw history.

***

The expansion draft welcomed the newest teams to Major League Baseball while reminding them of the daunting task ahead: starting from scratch with players left unprotected by their rivals, who were all established teams with fertile farm systems.

Still, three of the first four expansion teams fared as well as could be expected in their maiden seasons. The Los Angeles Angels finished 70–91 and in eighth place in the now-10-team American League. The Washington Senators were tied for last with the Kansas City Athletics at 61–100.

In 1962, the Houston Colt .45s finished eighth in the NL with a 64–96 record. They placed ahead of the oldest franchise in the sport, the Chicago Cubs, who ended the season 59–103.

And then, in 10th place, resided the New York Mets, who finished at 40–120—the worst record in baseball's modern era—and 60 ½ games out of first place. No team would finish even 45 games out of first place until 2003.

Three thousand miles away, the Giants and Dodgers were offering a glimpse at what could have been in New York. The former Big Apple residents finished the season tied for first place at 101–61. The Giants won a three-game playoff for the pennant. The winning pitcher in the decisive third game? Don Larsen.

As for the Mets, they acquired 41 players in the winter prior to their debut. Sixteen were discarded during the season. Roger Craig started the first game in franchise history but gave up three runs while committing a balk in the first inning against the St. Louis Cardinals. In the penultimate inning of the season finale, the Mets hit into a triple play.

The Mets lost their first nine games—and the Pittsburgh Pirates won their first 10 games, which meant the Mets were 9 ½ games out of first place before their first win. They later endured losing streaks of 17 games, 13 games, and 11 games. At one point, Stengel declared, "Can't anybody play this here game?"

Even as the Mets were setting records for futility, Stengel was helping to establish the franchise's identity. Despite the mounting losses,

Stengel was generally upbeat. He encouraged fans to come watch the team he called "amazin'," a moniker that would stick with the Mets until it was actually utilized in a nonironic fashion.

Though the home team usually lost, the fans attending games at the Polo Grounds—and, beginning in 1964, Shea Stadium—were supportive and treated the rare victories as cathartic moments to be enjoyed.

"I think most of the people in New York knew that we probably were not quite as talented as the other teams were, but the fact is we tried hard," says pitcher Jack Fisher, who joined the Mets in 1964. "And I think the fans saw that and appreciated it. And when we won a game, it was a big thing. They were absolutely great."

"We didn't have the old Dodgers/Giants fans," Hunt says. "We made them Mets fans.

"And I gave 'em 100 percent whether I did good or not, or looked like shit, or whatever."

Stengel also made it clear that any chance to vanquish the Yankees should be cherished. Of course, this was 35 years before interleague play, so head-to-head opportunities were limited to the occasional spring training game and, eventually, an in-season exhibition dubbed the Mayor's Trophy Game.

With the Yankees, Stengel managed 63 World Series games, including six Game Sevens. But still stinging from the fashion in which the Yankees dismissed him, Stengel approached his exhibitions against his former employer as if a championship were at stake.

"I'm so nervous, I don't know what to do with myself," Stengel said before the first Mayor's Trophy Game on June 20, 1963.

The Mets won, 6–2, at Yankee Stadium. They were 65–163 in regular-season games, but now they had intracity bragging rights. As Stan Isaacs wrote in *Newsday*: "It is a fact that nobody can deny. In the history of baseball games between the Mets and the Yankees in New York, the Mets lead 1–0."

Stengel was just as focused the next year, when the Yankees earned a 6–4 win at Shea Stadium on August 24. While Yankees manager Yogi

Berra sent minor league pitcher Jim Brenneman to the mound, Stengel shuffled his rotation so that he could pitch one of his most reliable starters in relief.

"Obviously, when Casey was the manager, that was a big game for him," Fisher says. "He wanted to win. I think I only pitched in one [Mayor's Trophy Game]. I came in relief. I think we were [playing] them here at Shea Stadium and it was on a Monday, I guess. I think I was starting on Wednesday, but Casey had me out in the bullpen."

Fisher laughed.

"And I came in and pitched an inning in the game," Fisher says.

Fisher's next scheduled start was pushed back two days.

The arrival of the Mets coincided with the beginning of the Yankees' downfall. The Yankees reached the World Series in each of their first four post-Stengel seasons, winning in 1961 and 1962 before falling in 1963 and 1964.

The latter loss represented the end of the Yankees' era of dominance. The Yankees had their first losing season in 40 years in 1965 and finished at least 20 games out of first place each season from 1965 to 1968.

The Mets fared even worse, going a combined 250–397 while finishing at least 24 games out of first place each year. Mets fans were far more patient than their crosstown brethren: over that four-year period, the Mets drew 7,048,231 fans to Shea Stadium—more than 500,000 more per year than the Yankees (4,783,380 fans) drew to Yankee Stadium.

In 1969, those Mets fans would be rewarded with the most stunning rags-to-riches story in sports history.

***

The 1969 Mets were the 18th team in the four major North American pro sports leagues to win a championship a season after finishing with a losing record. They mounted an impressive comeback from 10 games down in the National League East with 49 to play, but even that was not without precedent: just five years earlier, the St. Louis Cardinals were 11 games out of first place with 43 left to play before edging out the Philadelphia Phillies by a game.

Nor were the Mets even the first surprise New York champion of 1969. In January, Joe Namath guaranteed victory in Super Bowl III before the Jets stunned the football establishment by becoming the first AFL world champion with an upset of the NFL's Baltimore Colts.

But this unforeseen championship was different from any that came before it and would set the standard for all that followed. The Mets went 394–737 in their first seven seasons of existence, a span in which the team spent one single day over .500 (the 1966 squad improved to 2–1 with a win on April 17). They were trying to carve an identity—beyond that of a team that endeared in spite of its on-field pratfalls—in the biggest city in the world and in the shadow of the most decorated baseball team in the world.

In one season, the lovable losers turned into world champions. The Mets moved into first place for the first time ever on September 10 and ended up going 100–62 while winning the NL East by eight games over the Chicago Cubs. The Mets clinched the division with a 6–0 win over the St. Louis Cardinals on September 24, 1969, when a Cardinals cleanup hitter named Joe Torre hit into the game-ending double play.

The Mets then swept the Braves in the inaugural NL Championship Series before losing the first game of the World Series to the 109-win Baltimore Orioles. But the Mets won the next four games and sealed the championship with a final out that remains one of the most iconic scenes in baseball history.

With a runner on first and the Mets nursing a 5–3 lead, Davey Johnson, who would manage the Mets' second World Series-winning club 17 years later, hit a Jerry Koosman pitch to deep left field. A sellout crowd of 57,397 was roaring so loud that Koosman didn't hear the sound of Johnson's bat hitting the ball.

"I really had to look at Cleon [Jones] to see his reaction to it," Koosman said afterward. "When I saw him go back just about to the warning track and then stop, I knew that the ball was in the ballpark."

The ball indeed came down just shy of the warning track, where Jones settled and caught it. As the ball landed in his glove, fans began storming the field—and Jones, as longtime *Newsday* Mets beat writer Marty Noble described it in 2000 while listing the final out of the Series as the greatest moment in Mets history, ". . . bends a knee as if he has undergone a religious experience."

The Mets might have stunned the world with their resurrection. But the players weren't surprised by their rise.

"We didn't wear skirts—Cinderella wore a skirt, didn't she?" Koosman says. "You've got to talk to Gil Hodges. Go up there and talk to Gil Hodges."

Like many original Mets, Hodges was in the decline phase of his career when he was selected by the club in the 1961 expansion draft. Unlike the rest of his teammates, Hodges was synonymous with baseball in New York. He spent the first 16 years of his career with the Dodgers, a span so long it included a two-year, Bronze Star-winning stint with the Marine Corps during World War II and ended with Hodges accompanying the Dodgers to Los Angeles for their first four seasons in California.

Hodges finished his career by playing in 65 games for the Mets from 1962 to 1963 before he was traded to the Washington Senators, where he promptly became their manager. After four-plus sub-.500 seasons as the Senators' skipper, Hodges was fired but immediately hired by the Mets to become their third full-time manager after Stengel, who retired after breaking his hip during the 1965 season, and Wes Westrum.

Hodges made it clear from the moment he arrived he had no interest in overseeing a group of players known as lovable losers. The Mets went 73–89 in 1968, but Hodges had already begun building a foundation for success with a promising young core of homegrown players.

"That first year, he took all us pitchers, along with Eddie Yost, the third base coach, and went over to the other little field," says Koosman, who teamed up with future Hall of Famer Tom Seaver to headline a powerful rotation. "He said, 'Now, a lot of you guys learned how to bunt in different organizations. But what we're going to do now is you're going to forget everything you learned.' He said, 'We're going to learn how to bunt my way.'

"And he taught us how he wanted us to bunt, and we were the best bunters in the league because we learned the Dodgers way. The Dodgers had the best basics in baseball of any team and they kept that tradition going."

Koosman spoke in a conference room located across the hall from a wall with a picture of Hodges and a quote attributed to the manager: "Just do the best with what you have and you'll soon be doing it better."

"Practice doesn't make perfect," Koosman says. "Perfect practice makes perfect."

The Mets followed up their championship season with back-to-back 83–79 campaigns. Despite missing the playoffs, there was little doubt they'd developed a winning identity under Hodges, who was turning into the face of the franchise, much like Stengel and Joe McCarthy had been with the Yankees and Walter Alston had been with the Dodgers.

But the Hodges era came to a tragic end on April 2, 1972, when Hodges died of a heart attack just two days shy of his 48th birthday. The heavy smoker, who had already survived one heart attack, collapsed after finishing a round of golf with his coaches and died almost immediately.

Hodges's death saddened the entire sport but hit New York—and the men who played for its past and present franchises—particularly hard. About 10,000 people attended Hodges's wake, which was held on what would have been his birthday. Jackie Robinson called Hodges the core of the Brooklyn Dodgers and told Gil Hodges Jr. that Gil Sr.'s wake was the worst day of his life outside the day his son died.

Yogi Berra, who joined the Mets' coaching staff after being fired as the Yankees' manager following the 1964 campaign, replaced Hodges as manager and oversaw another winning season for the Mets, who finished 83–73 and in third place in the NL East.

In 1973, Berra and the Mets authored a worthy sequel to their miraculous 1969 season. This time, the Mets were 13 games under .500 and mired in last place in the NL East in August, when Berra uttered perhaps his most famous Yogiism—"It ain't over till it's over"—and reliever Tug McGraw bellowed, "Ya gotta believe!"

The Mets ended the season on a 29–13 run to win the division with an 82–79 record—the worst record ever, at the time, for a playoff team. After stunning the Cincinnati Reds and their budding "Big Red Machine" in a five-game NL Championship Series, the Mets came within a game of knocking off the dynastic Oakland Athletics in the World Series before losing Games Six and Seven.

As it turned out, though, the most notable New York baseball event—the one that would heighten the Mets-Yankees rivalry for the next three-plus decades—happened much earlier in 1973.

***

The worst decade in Yankees history happened to be the one in which the team was owned by CBS, which purchased the franchise from Del Webb and Dan Topping for $14 million following the 1964 season. While the Mets completed their stunning ascension, the Yankees never made the playoffs under their corporate ownership. CBS sensed the unhappiness of fans and agreed to sell the team in January 1973 to a group headed by a 42-year-old Ohio resident named George Steinbrenner, who'd made his fortune in the family shipping business.

Steinbrenner and his partners bought the Yankees for $10 million—a total that fell to $8.8 million once New York City bought a pair of nearby parking lots from the new owners.

"CBS came to the conclusion that perhaps it was not as viable for the network to own the Yankees as for some people," a CBS spokesman told *Sports Illustrated*. "Fans get worked up over great men, not great

**Photos by Rob Cuni, unless otherwise noted.**

Bobby Valentine and Joe Torre's paths intersected long before they engaged in nightly chess matches during the 2000 World Series. A year later, both men, their teams, and their home stadiums would play pivotal roles in the healing effort for post-9/11 New York City.

The fevered Roger Clemens-Mike Piazza rivalry reached unimaginable levels during Game Two of the 2000 World Series. Two games later, David Cone made his final appearance in a Yankees uniform a memorable one by retiring Piazza in perhaps the biggest at-bat of the series.

Derek Jeter cemented his reputation as the most clutch player of his generation with a series of big hits during an MVP-winning performance in the 2000 World Series. His fellow "Core Four" members Jorge Posada and Bernie Williams scored the winning run in Game Five and caught the final out, respectively.

*Tom Hauck /Allsport*

Mets first baseman Todd Zeile hit .400 during the 2000 World Series but also missed hitting a pair of potentially series-changing homers by about five feet combined. He also teamed up with third baseman Robin Ventura, his close friend, to help set the tone for a mature, veteran clubhouse.

*Ezra Shaw/ALLSPORT*

*David Leeds / Allsport*

Top: Edgardo Alfonzo's prime would be cut short by chronic back troubles, but in 2000, a case could be made he was the best player in New York. Bottom: Tino Martinez succeeded a legend in Don Mattingly—and promptly helped spark a dynasty.

Mariano Rivera was well on his way to establishing himself as the most dominant closer—in playoffs and otherwise—of all time by 2000. But Jay Payton will always be able to say he was the second and last player to homer off Rivera in a postseason game.

While the Yankees were filled with superstars, the Mets' core was made up of overlooked players like Benny Agbayani, a Hawaii native and 30th-round draft pick; oft-injured former first-round pick Jay Payton; and utilityman Joe McEwing, who was a 28th-round draft pick.

*Jed Jacobsohn/ALLSPORT*

New Jersey native Al Leiter overcame numerous arm injuries early in his career to become the ace for his favorite childhood team. Texas native Andy Pettitte disproved those who thought he might be too nice off the field to become the Yankees' most dependable starting pitcher of the dynasty. The two southpaws engaged in intense battles during Games One and Five of the 2000 World Series.

corporations. We came to the realization, I think, that sports franchises really flourish better with people owning them."

The point person for the group that now owned the Yankees declared he and his partners would be hands-off owners.

"We plan absentee ownership as far as running the Yankees is concerned," Steinbrenner said at a press conference. "We're not going to pretend we're something we aren't. I'll stick to building ships."

He did not.

Manager Ralph Houk "resigned" at the end of the 1973 season. It was the first of 21 managerial changes to take place under Steinbrenner, who also hired and fired 12 general managers and countless public relations managers and other lower-level employees.

Much of Steinbrenner's chaos would yield the championships he demanded. But first, he had to share a stadium with the team over whom he'd obsess more than any other.

While Ebbets Field and the Polo Grounds met the wrecking ball shortly after the Dodgers and Giants went west, Yankee Stadium—built in 1923—continued to host the Yankees with minimal renovations until the 1970s, when the facility's state of disrepair could be ignored no longer.

In 1971, after the Yankees had engaged in negotiations with New Jersey about building a potential stadium in the Garden State, New York City announced plans to buy the Stadium from its owners—Rice University, located in Texas, and the Knights of Columbus—and oversee its renovations. In return, the Yankees would sign a 30-year lease with the city.

The lease agreement was finally reached near the end of the 1972 season. The city would complete the renovations in time for the 1976 season. That, of course, left the Yankees with no place to play in 1974 and 1975.

New York City, of course, had a place: Shea Stadium.

The Yankees had no interest in being the Mets' guests, and the Mets had no interest in hosting the Yankees. But since New York City owned both stadia, neither side had a say in the matter.

"Two baseball clubs have never worked well in the same stadium," Mets president Donald M. Grant told the *New York Times* in 1971. "I don't think [Yankees president] Michael Burke wants to have his team in Shea Stadium any more than we want ours in Yankee Stadium. Would you like to give a very important party in my house?"

Grant also acknowledged he was still displeased with the Yankees for not making Yankee Stadium available to the expansion Mets, who ended up playing their first two seasons in the outdated Polo Grounds.

"What did they ever do for us?" Grant said.

Steinbrenner may have been wondering the same thing. Yankees reliever Sparky Lyle wrote in *The Bronx Zoo*—his memoir of the 1978 season—that Steinbrenner didn't like the Mets because they refused to share with the Yankees the profits from concessions and parking at Shea Stadium in 1974–75 and limited the number of Yankees grounds crew personnel that could work at Shea.

But other than the Yankees nearly burning Shea down in June 1975—the team was honoring the 200th anniversary of the Army with a 21-gun salute when one of the shots landed in center field and set the fence on fire—the two rivals were able to share the building without incident for two seasons, even though neither team really liked the arrangement.

"It just didn't seem right, just because we were the Yankees," former Yankees Manager Bill Virdon told author Brett Topel in the book *When Shea Was Home*. "You lived with it, because that was life."

"I don't know what it would be like to share a ball field with somebody else," former Mets reliever Skip Lockwood says. "But we weren't using it on the road, so I guess it was all right."

Yankee Stadium reopened just in time for the home tenant to begin another mini-dynasty. The Yankees returned to the World Series in 1976, when they fell to the Reds in four games, before winning back-to-back championships over the Dodgers.

Between their on-field success and off-field drama, the Yankees generated the attention Steinbrenner craved in New York City and beyond.

Steinbrenner, who was suspended from baseball for two years (a sentence later reduced to nine months) after pleading guilty in 1974 to making illegal contributions to the reelection campaign of President Richard Nixon two years earlier, signed Reggie Jackson to a five-year deal following the 1976 season.

The marriage of the egocentric Jackson and combustible manager Billy Martin was a heavenly one for the tabloids. Jackson reportedly (though he later denied saying it) told *Sport* magazine in the June 1977 issue that he was ". . . the straw that stirs the drink" and that Yankees captain Thurman Munson ". . . thinks he can be the straw that stirs the drink, but he can only stir it bad."

June was an eventful month for Jackson and Martin, who nearly fought each other in the cramped visitor's dugout at Fenway Park on June 18 after Martin pulled Jackson in the middle of an inning for not appearing to run hard after a bloop double by Jim Rice.

The Yankees overcame their infighting and won the World Series, but Martin stepped down due to what he called health reasons on July 24, 1978. Five days later, Martin was introduced at Old Timers Day as the Yankees' manager-in-waiting for 1980. The Yankees ended up winning their second straight title under Bob Lemon, who was fired 64 games into the 1979 season and replaced by Martin, who was fired himself in October shortly after he got into a fight with a marshmallow salesman in Minnesota. This, of course, meant he was hired and fired before the 1980 season in which he was supposed to return to the dugout.

The Mets were positively milquetoast by comparison. Beginning in 1977, when backup infielder Joe Torre took over as player/manager on May 31 before retiring as a player less than a month later, the Mets endured seven straight losing seasons. Torre was fired following the 1981 season having lost 134 more games than he won as a manager.

But Steinbrenner remained obsessed with retaining bragging rights over the Mets. This meant treating the annual Mayor's Trophy Game exhibition with the reverence usually reserved for the World Series.

By 1978, the curiosity factor was long gone from the midseason Mets-Yankees game. Only 9,792 people—the smallest crowd in Mayor's Trophy history—turned out to Yankee Stadium to see the Yankees earn a 4–3, 13-inning win. Those in attendance saw the Yankees start sore-armed veteran Catfish Hunter, as well as third baseman Graig Nettles try to literally throw the game away once extra innings arrived.

"In the dugout, Nettles said to me, 'If I get a ball hit to me, I'm going to let it beat against my chest, and I'm going to throw it into the stands,'" Lyle wrote in *The Bronx Zoo*.

Nettles indeed airmailed a throw to first base on a routine grounder by Mets catcher Ron Hodges, but much to Lyle's apparent displeasure, the Mets never scored the tie-breaking run.

In 2011, Lyle and Nettles both told the *Wall Street Journal* there was no attempt to throw the game.

"Was there a chance he did it? Hell, no," Lyle said. "Anybody who knows Graig Nettles knows he's not going to do that in a Mayor's Trophy game or a [bleeping] beer-league game or anything else. It was just something we were joking about because the Mets were pretty bad at that time."

There would be just five more Mayor's Trophy games before the series was discontinued in 1983.

The Yankees and Mets came closer than ever to being out there against each other for real in the mid-1980s.

The Mets' rebuilding effort began to bear fruit in 1983, when outfielder Darryl Strawberry won the Rookie of the Year award. In 1984, under first-year manager Davey Johnson, the Mets went 90–72 behind homegrown players such as Strawberry and 19-year-old pitcher Dwight Gooden, who won the Rookie of the Year by going 17–9 with a 2.60 ERA and a major league-leading 276 strikeouts.

The Yankees, meanwhile, had a young star of their own in second-year first baseman Don Mattingly, who won the batting title with a

.343 average for a team that finished 87–75, marking just the sixth time both New York teams finished with a winning record in the same season.

Finally, fans of both teams had a legitimate claim to bragging rights. The arguments carried on in offices, barrooms, and on school playgrounds throughout the tri-state area: who was better?

"The fans would compare the players," Strawberry says. "Donnie was great. [Mets first baseman] Keith [Hernandez] was great. [Yankees ace Ron] Guidry was great. Doc was great."

Every spring began with New York City hoping for a Subway Series in the fall, but for the first time since the Mets were born, a Big Apple-based World Series seemed possible as 1985 dawned.

The Mets acquired Gary Carter from the Expos in hopes the veteran catcher would be the missing piece. While Carter hit a career-high 32 homers and collected 100 RBIs, Gooden led the Mets' pursuit of a division title, following up his spectacular rookie season with one of the greatest performances of all-time: A Cy Young Award-winning campaign in which he went 24–4 with a 1.52 ERA.

The Yankees fell into a quick hole in the AL East—after opening 6–10, Steinbrenner fired Yogi Berra, fracturing a relationship that wouldn't heal for another 15 years, and hired Martin for a third time. The team nevertheless surged into contention behind Mattingly, who won the Most Valuable Player award by hitting .324 with 35 homers and a major league-leading 145 RBIs.

By the final weekend of the season, both the Mets and Yankees had more than 95 wins but were in second place behind the St. Louis Cardinals and Toronto Blue Jays, respectively. While the Mets had to sweep the Montreal Expos and hope the Cardinals lost at least twice to the Chicago Cubs, the Yankees visited the Blue Jays knowing a sweep would force a one-game playoff.

Both New York teams won Friday, but they lost within half an hour of each other Saturday—the Mets followed the Yankees—to fall out of contention. The Mets finished with 98 wins and the Yankees ended at

97 wins—the third- and fourth-most victories in baseball—but headed home in the pre-wild card era. They were only the sixth and seventh teams in the division era to miss the playoffs with at least 97 wins.

Still, optimism remained high, inside and outside clubhouses, that a Subway Series was imminent.

"Both teams would take that—play in a Subway Series, not have to travel," Mattingly says with a grin. "It's something that all the guys would like, because that means that you've had success enough to get the World Series and then you're home. Any kind of rivalry like that is going to create such a good buzz."

But while the Yankees finished second again in 1986, the Mets completed their ascension—Steinbrenner's worst nightmare—as a hard-edged, hard-living team barreling its way to 108 wins and the pennant before facing the Boston Red Sox, Steinbrenner's other must-beat foe, in a classic World Series.

The Red Sox were one pitch away from winning the championship in Game Six 16 times, but the Mets mounted a stunning comeback that ended with Mookie Wilson's slow roller up the first base line glancing off Bill Buckner's glove and Ray Knight racing home with the winning run, his hands on his helmet as if he couldn't believe what was happening. The Mets then came back from a three-run deficit to win Game Seven.

The remainder of the '80s and the start of the '90s would be defined by diminishing returns for each team. The Yankees, increasingly hamstrung by Steinbrenner's win-now trades and mounting failures on the free agent market, fell to fourth place in 1987 and to fifth place in 1988 before enduring just their second losing season in 16 years in 1989 and finishing in last place in 1990. The four losing seasons the Yankees had from 1989 through 1992 marked the first time the franchise finished under .500 in four straight seasons since 1912–15.

The Mets never became the dynasty many expected and made the playoffs just once more—they fell to the Los Angeles Dodgers in a seven-game NLCS in 1988—before falling under .500 in 1991.

After Strawberry left as a free agent following the 1990 season, ownership tried to pull a page from Steinbrenner's book by signing and acquiring a bevy of big names. But there was no Catfish Hunter or Reggie Jackson to be found amongst the likes of Bobby Bonilla, Vince Coleman, Eddie Murray, or Bret Saberhagen, all of whom chafed under the bright lights of the Big Apple.

The Mets bottomed out in 1993, when they went 59–103 during a season in which Saberhagen sprayed bleach on a group of reporters and Coleman was arrested after three people, including two children, were injured when he threw a lit firecracker into a crowd following a game at Dodger Stadium.

As the Mets endured their first 100-loss season in more than a quarter century, the Yankees' first true rebuilding effort in generations began to pay off. The suspension of Steinbrenner—who received a "lifetime ban" from baseball in 1990 for paying gambler Howie Spira $40,000 to unearth dirt on the charity operated by Yankees outfielder Dave Winfield—allowed general manager Gene Michael to draft and/or keep prospects such as Derek Jeter, Andy Pettitte, Bernie Williams, Jorge Posada, and Mariano Rivera as well as acquire veterans such as Paul O'Neill, David Cone, and Wade Boggs.

Steinbrenner's ban was lifted in 1993, when the Yankees went 88–74 and finished second in the AL East behind the World Series-winning Blue Jays. The Yankees were in first place when the player's strike ended the 1994 season in August and finally snapped their 14-year playoff drought—the longest in franchise history—when they clinched the wild card on the final day of the 1995 season.

In 1996, the last bit of bragging rights enjoyed by Mets fans disappeared. Under first-year manager Joe Torre, the Yankees returned to the top by winning their first World Series in 18 years—the team's longest drought in more than 70 years. The Mets finished 71–91 and underwent their fourth managerial change of the decade August 26, when Dallas Green was fired and replaced by Triple-A Norfolk manager Bobby Valentine.

But long before Charlie Hayes squeezed the last out of the Yankees' championship, fans of both teams already knew they'd soon get a chance to argue in real time over whose team was better in a head-to-head setting.

In January 1996, baseball's owners voted unanimously to implement regular-season interleague play beginning in 1997. For the first time, the American League and the National League would share a diamond in something other than an All-Star Game or World Series.

Purists blanched at the departure from the norm and believed commissioner Bud Selig was selling out the traditions of the game in an attempt to appeal to younger fans and/or win back fans who left the sport following the strike of 1994. Other critics believed interleague play would diminish the impact of the World Series if the two teams already played each other earlier in the season—a suggestion shrugged off by Selig.

"There's nothing in the Constitution of the United States that forbids that," Selig said after the owners held their vote. "I remember sitting at the Super Bowl last year and watching San Francisco play San Diego and somebody said they played last November. There was no less interest."

He'd be proven right about that in four years. It didn't take nearly that long for interleague play to become a hit in New York City.

A sellout crowd of 56,188 filled Yankee Stadium on June 16, 1997, to watch the long-awaited first regular-season clash between the reigning World Series champion Yankees and the perpetually downtrodden Mets be dominated by . . . the Mets and Dave Mlicki?

The 28-year-old right-hander took the mound that Monday night with a 4.70 ERA in his first 13 starts of the season and an overall big-league record of 17–21 with a 4.12 ERA dating back to 1992. But the Mets staked him to a three-run lead in the first inning—the slow-footed duo of Todd Hundley and Butch Huskey executed a double steal, with Hundley swiping home, to score the third run—and Mlicki scattered nine hits in his first career shutout as the Mets cruised to a 6–0 win.

The fans brought with them an energy not often associated with weeknight midseason games.

"That was intense," Hundley says. "Every single pitch, it was either half of them standing up and cheering or the other half booing.

"They went the whole series like that. We played [three] games like that and it was incredible. The most intense games."

Even more intense games, of course, were to be played in three years. But while the Yankees' core for the 2000 Subway Series was already in place for the inaugural clash between the rivals—the 2000 team had 11 players remaining from the 1997 squad, including seven who would eventually be honored with a plaque in Monument Park—only eight of the 25 Mets who played in the 2000 World Series were in the organization for that first interleague series.

None of them made it to Cooperstown, and only John Franco was honored with induction into the Mets Hall of Fame. All of which meant they were the perfect holdovers for a mismatched general manager-manager tandem who had in common a soft spot for the overlooked and the underappreciated.

On July 16, 1997, exactly four weeks after the Mets-Yankees series concluded, Mets owner Fred Wilpon fired General Manager Joe McIlvaine and replaced him with Assistant General Manager Steve Phillips.

"The function of a general manager has changed dramatically," Wilpon said. "The 'skill set' of a Steve Phillips matches what a GM should be."

The hiring of Phillips indeed put the Mets at the forefront of a front office revolution. Phillips was young (34), well educated (he had a degree in psychology from Michigan), and had experience in the corporate arena. After retiring as a player in 1988, he spent a little more than a year working for Maritz Motivational Company, which was based in St. Louis and consulted with Fortune 500 companies.

But the former elite athlete who starred in three sports at his

Michigan high school and turned down a scholarship to play football at Northwestern in order to sign with the Mets out of high school—he was selected in the fifth round of the 1981 draft, three rounds before the Mets took Lenny Dykstra and seven rounds before they picked Roger Clemens—realized he missed baseball, even though he'd found his six-year minor league career a torturous experience.

"Playing for me was painful—I didn't deal very well with failure," Phillips says. "I could take batting practice and take extra hitting and I'd hit nine balls right on the button, drive them to the gap. And then the 10th one, I'd pop up and I would feel the pain of the one bad swing."

One day after Phillips told his then-fiancée he'd like to get into a baseball front office, McIlvaine called Phillips and asked if he'd be interested in an administrative assistant job with the minor league scouting department. Phillips returned to the Mets in January 1990. By September 1991, he was named the team's director of minor leagues, a position he held until being promoted to assistant general manager in December 1995.

The six seasons dealing with the Mets' prospects allowed Phillips to utilize the broad spectrum of experience he'd gained during his own playing career, which peaked at Double-A.

"I was a prospect, then I was a suspect, and then I was a guy that was filling out the roster for the prospects to play," Phillips said in 1999. "I was traded. I was released. I had the chance to be a six-year minor league free agent. I've experienced most of the emotions players experience and I think that ability to empathize with what the player goes through on a daily basis has been very helpful."

In that regard, Phillips had a lot in common with Valentine, who was one of the finest high school athletes in Connecticut history. At the time of his graduation in 1968, Valentine held the state records for touchdowns (53) as well as the fastest time in the 60-yard dash. He was offered a scholarship to the University of Southern California to replace running back O.J. Simpson, who had just graduated, but chose to sign with the Los Angeles Dodgers, who made him the fifth pick of the 1968 draft.

According to the *Hartford Courant*, Dodgers scouting director Al Campanis declared Valentine ". . . could be the best baseball player in America." Valentine initially met expectations by winning MVP awards at rookie-level Ogden in 1968, when he became close friends with future Dodgers manager Tommy Lasorda, and by making his big-league debut in 1969. He won another MVP, this time at Triple-A Spokane, in 1970.

But a torn-up knee in 1971 slowed Valentine's ascension. The Dodgers traded Valentine to the California Angels prior to the 1973 season, and his career all but came to a halt on May 17, when he suffered a grotesque leg injury while trying to make a catch at the center-field wall. Valentine's right leg got stuck in the wall while the rest of him did not. He suffered multiple fractures and was left, as described by the *Courant* in 1999, with a 17-degree bend between his right knee and ankle.

Valentine played on one good leg for four more teams until the end of the decade. He was a utilityman with the Mets under Joe Torre in 1977 and 1978 before ending his career with the Seattle Mariners in 1979.

" I was the best player on my team, and broke my leg," Valentine says. "And then I became the worst player on the team. So I had a perspective I don't know that many people ever have. I understood what it was to be the most touted, and understood what it was to be the easiest forgotten as a player."

A decade after he appeared to be headed to stardom as a player, Valentine embarked upon another fast track, this time to the dugout as a manager. He worked as a minor league infield instructor for the San Diego Padres in 1980 and 1981 before taking the same job with the Mets in 1982, where one of the minor leaguers he met was Phillips, a second-year infielder at Single-A Little Falls.

"He was the best coach I ever had," Phillips says. "He could push the buttons that you needed pushed to feel good about yourself. He was hard-working, he was positive, he had good energy. I always loved him when I was playing."

After the season, Valentine was promoted to the Mets' big-league coaching staff, where he stayed until May 16, 1985, when, three days after his 35th birthday, Valentine was named the manager of the Texas Rangers.

The Rangers had just six winning seasons in their first 25 years of existence before Valentine directed them to four winning season in his first six years at the helm. Texas was 45–41 when Valentine was fired July 9, 1992. The Rangers finished 77–85.

Valentine went to the Cincinnati Reds in 1993 and became the Mets' Triple-A manager in 1994. The next year, he went to Japan to manage the Chiba Lotte Marines, who had finished in last place 15 straight seasons. Only one American had ever managed a team in Japan, but Don Blasingame spent a dozen seasons in Japan as a player and a coach before becoming a manager in the 1970s. Valentine would be the first foreigner to attempt to manage in Japan without ever playing or coaching a game overseas.

"Chiba Lotte had been a managers' graveyard," Valentine told the *Los Angeles Times*. "No one in Japan wanted the job. They had tried everything."

Valentine once again helped turn a franchise around, this time guiding the Marines to a second-place finish in the Pacific Division. Following the season finale, Marines fans showered Valentine with a curtain call.

But barely a month later, Valentine received a call at his Connecticut home informing him the Marines were firing him despite the fact he was signed for the 1996 season. Valentine was told he was fired because of the cultural gap. Even with his success, his methodology—which included allowing players to skip the daily four-hour batting practice sessions in order to conserve their strength for the games—was unacceptable in a society built on rigorous adherence to the norms.

Once again, Valentine didn't have to wait long to find another job.

He'd just returned home from being fired when he received a phone call from Phillips. Five years after McIlvaine had brought home Phillips, the latter was about to bring Valentine back by offering him a second go-around as the manager at Triple-A Norfolk.

When McIlvaine was fired and replaced by Phillips with the Mets in the midst of a winning season in 1997, conspiracy theorists suggested Valentine helped execute the move in the shadows. The volatility of the Phillips-Valentine relationship would soon disprove those allegations. But there was no denying Phillips had an uncanny knack for acquiring the type of battle-scarred players who would thrive under Valentine's tutelage.

"I always had a lot of respect for those guys who would grind it out, because I was one, too," Phillips says. "Those guys who were sort of workers and maybe less of a superstar, or more of the soldiers and the worker bees—I think I had an affinity for those type of guys."

Phillips made his first deal as general manager on August 8, 1997, when he traded Lance Johnson and two players to be named later to the Chicago Cubs in exchange for Brian McRae, Mel Rojas, and Turk Wendell, the latter of whom was 30 years old, had a 4.41 big league ERA, and was better known for his superstitions than anything he'd done on the mound. Wendell jumped over the foul line as he walked to and from the mound—a habit born when he touched the foul lines before giving up runs in a high school game—and spent his time between innings eating licorice and brushing his teeth.

In other words, as someone with a quirky backstory that followed him everywhere he went regardless of how well he performed, Wendell was going to fit in well with the holdovers from the pre-Phillips era.

Wendell's new teammates included utility infielder Matt Franco, who was acquired by the Mets in 1996 and remained best known as the nephew of actor Kurt Russell until July 10, 1999, when Franco laced a two-run pinch-hit RBI single off Mariano Rivera to give the Mets a walk-off 9–8 win.

Pitcher Rick Reed, signed by the Mets as a minor league free agent following the 1996 season, was known for serving as a replacement player in spring training during the 1995 strike. Backup catcher Todd Pratt signed with the Mets following a 1995 season in which he didn't play professional ball and instead split his time between working at a baseball academy operated by ex-Yankees shortstop Bucky Dent and delivering pizzas for Domino's. Pitcher Bobby Jones, a first-round pick of the Mets in 1991, went 74–56 with a 4.13 ERA for the Mets and was better known for being born in Fresno, California, just like the greatest Met in franchise history, Tom Seaver.

Even the most decorated of the holdovers did not have an easy path to becoming a key part of a World Series-bound team. Edgardo Alfonzo placed in the top 15 in the NL Most Valuable Player balloting three times from 1997 through 2000, but before that he was viewed as a utility player within his own organization. Future Mets Hall of Famer John Franco became the NL's all-time saves leader in 1997, but the fast-talking, undersized Brooklyn native did it with a changeup-screwball combination and an uncanny knack for getting into and out of his own jams.

"It was kind of a working man's team, it was the blue-collar team," Todd Zeile says. "We had a lot of parts that gelled well together. We believed that we could win. We believed that we were as good as anybody that we faced."

Phillips began adding to the Mets' core following the 1997 season, when he found Wendell's left-handed doppelgänger in Dennis Cook, whom he acquired from the Florida Marlins in exchange for a pair of minor leaguers. Cook had already played for seven teams and bounced between the rotation and the bullpen before establishing himself as a reliable situational southpaw.

Phillips again did business with the rebuilding Marlins in February 1998, when he sent three more minor leaguers to Florida in exchange for left-handed starter Al Leiter. The New Jersey native made just 13 big-league appearances from 1989 through 1992 as he battled a series of arm injuries, but he'd won 53 games and two World Series rings in the previous five seasons.

In May 1998, Phillips made the biggest trade of his career, yet again with the Marlins, when he dealt another trio of minor leaguers for Mike Piazza, the Hall of Fame-bound catcher who began his career as a 62nd-round draft pick.

Over the next 26 months, Phillips continued building a championship-caliber club built almost entirely out of players whose nonlinear paths to New York matched those of their new manager and general manager. He did so even as the relationship between him and Valentine continued to fray.

Valentine believed things changed following the general manager's meetings in 1998. Phillips was on a leave of absence following the acknowledgment of an affair he'd had with a Mets employee. In his stead, the Mets sent Frank Cashen, the general manager of the World Series-winning 1986 team, to direct a group that included all of Phillips's assistants as well as Valentine, who said he tried to take a leadership role and implore the rest of the group to focus on their new jobs instead of when or if Phillips would return.

"They're saying, 'Well, so what do you think about Steve? What have you heard?'" Valentine says. "And I said to them 'Fuck Steve, we have work to do right here. I don't want to hear another word about Steve, because he's not here.'

"And then the next thing I know, Steve calls me in and accuses me of trying to be the general manager."

Phillips, who returned to the team shortly after the meetings, said he didn't think Valentine was trying to take his job during his absence and that the only person he was mad at was himself.

"Obviously, I put everybody in a bad position during that time and people had to sort of step up and take on responsibilities that wouldn't necessarily have been theirs," Phillips says. "I don't blame anybody for what they would have gone through at that point. I'm the only one that deserved any blame during that period of time."

Phillips said he couldn't point to one instance of why his relationship with Valentine changed. He theorized maybe it was a matter of working in New York, where the already complicated tasks of building a championship baseball team were magnified by the size of the city and the shadow cast by the rival across town.

"Part of you is just trying to survive the job in New York," Phillips says. "And then there's part of you trying to do what you can to win in New York. But you always felt like you were fighting for your life and your career, your job."

Upon returning to his office, Phillips resumed putting together what would become the 2000 World Series team. On December 1, Phillips signed third baseman Robin Ventura, a dual-threat third baseman who overcame a career-threatening broken ankle in 1997, to a four-year deal. On the same day, he also traded for Armando Benitez, a flame-throwing right-hander in need of a fresh start after his instigation of a brawl with the Yankees left him alienated from his Baltimore Orioles teammates.

Twenty days later, Phillips signed Pat Mahomes, who'd spent the previous season-and-a-half in Japan after posting a 5.88 ERA in the majors from 1992 through 1997.

Darryl Hamilton, a 34-year-old who'd played for four teams in the previous five seasons, was acquired in a deadline deal in July 1999. Glendon Rusch, a once-hyped prospect who had struggled in parts of three seasons with the Kansas City Royals, arrived via a seemingly minor trade (the Mets gave up pitcher Dan Murray, who pitched one game in New York) two months later.

After the Mets came within two wins of the World Series in 1999—a season in which the Mets started 27–28 before Phillips fired three of Valentine's coaches during a Subway Series at Yankee Stadium—Phillips signed Todd Zeile, who played three positions for seven different teams over the previous four years, to play first base regularly for the first time in his career.

On December 22, Phillips pulled off a blockbuster trade with the

Houston Astros in which he acquired 22-game winner Mike Hampton as well as outfielder Derek Bell, a former 20/20 player coming off the worst season of his career.

With the key players in place, Phillips spent the first seven months of 2000 tinkering. He signed free agent utilityman Kurt Abbott shortly before spring training and added another jack-of-all trades, Joe McEwing, via a spring training trade with the St. Louis Cardinals. (The return for McEwing: Jesse Orosco, who recorded the final out of the Mets' 1986 World Series win.) Few noticed on March 27, when the Mets purchased outfielder Timo Perez from Hiroshima in the Japan Central League and assigned him to their Triple-A club.

Everyone noticed on April 14, when Phillips flew to Pittsburgh to confront Valentine over comments he made during a trip to the University of Pennsylvania's Wharton School of Business, where Valentine delivered a speech on the business of baseball.

While Valentine made it clear during his speech that he didn't agree with all the moves Phillips made, he didn't say anything out of the ordinary until afterward, when three fans in Mets jerseys approached Valentine as he walked the campus. One fan asked Valentine why the Mets signed light-hitting shortstop Rey Ordonez to a four-year deal during the off-season and why the team acquired Bell.

"I facetiously said, 'Because we wanted to pay the guy with the lowest on-base and slugging percentage in the history of baseball and we wanted to reward him,'" Valentine says. "And they said, 'Why in the world would you get a guy like Derek Bell?' And I said, 'I guess it's because I think Benny's [Agbayani] a better player and now he's not going to get a chance to play.'

"We're just walking and talking. Turns out the kid has a blog."

One of the fans—who identified himself as "Brad34"—posted Valentine's comments on a message board at the Mets' official website. By the time the Mets got to Pittsburgh to face the Pirates, Valentine's comments were national news and Phillips was at Three Rivers Stadium waiting to speak to Valentine, who held on to his job when Phillips was able to ascertain Valentine had made the comments not in a speech, but in what he believed to be an off-the-record session.

"Look, the thing that made Bobby great was his passion and his energy and knowledge of the game," Phillips says. "The thing that got Bobby in trouble once in a while was his passion and his energy and his knowledge of the game."

Phillips continued to add players throughout the middle of the 2000 season. Lenny Harris, who ended the 1998 season with the club before departing as a free agent, was reacquired in June for former top prospect Bill Pulsipher.

The arrival of Harris, who was beloved during his first stint with the team, added a new layer to a unique leadership group. The Mets' best players—Alfonzo, Piazza, Zeile, and Ventura—were universally well liked and respected inside the locker room, but all four were the type of players who led by a stoic and workmanlike example.

None were naturally vocal types, which allowed the boisterous duo of Harris and Todd Pratt—the latter of whom was nicknamed "Tank," which seemed appropriate given his broad physique and booming voice—to take on those leadership duties.

"Whoever was pitching, me or Todd would say something like, 'Man, this guy don't have a chance, we've got to get to this guy early,'" Harris says. "You always try to motivate your team to get ready to win a ball game. And I think that was one of the most important things I did when I was here, because we had too much of a good team to lose. I thought we had everything."

On July 28, Phillips picked up the final pieces in a pair of deals. First, he acquired Mike Bordick from the Baltimore Orioles to man shortstop in place of the injured Rey Ordonez. Bordick reached the bigs as an undrafted free agent out of the University of Maine and eventually replaced Hall of Fame ironman Cal Ripken Jr. as the Orioles' shortstop.

Later in the day, Phillips obtained bench bat Bubba Trammell and right-handed reliever Rick White from the Tampa Bay Devil Rays.

Trammell never played regularly for the fledgling Devil Rays despite batting .285 with 33 homers in 207 games. White, meanwhile, was having one of the best seasons of any American League reliever but was peppered with questions about his David Wells-esque appearance and previous off-season employment as a bouncer.

Ventura greeted the newcomers the next morning by buying a package of name tags and distributing them to Bordick, Trammell, and White, who affixed the tags to their clothing. A few hours later, Bordick homered on the first pitch he saw with the Mets, and White earned the win in his debut as the Mets beat the Cardinals.

"His first pitch he hits out of the park," White said afterward. "And my first inning, I get a win and help us win a game. Can't write it down any better than that."

The puzzle comprised of overlooked misfits and castoffs was complete.

"I think the path that a lot of individuals on that club had taken to get there—you understand the grind of everything, the grind of everyday, of what it takes to be the 25th guy on a team, to be the number-one player on a team," says McEwing, the 25th man. "You're talking about a 62nd-round draft pick as the number-one player on the team.

"It all meshed."

***

Prior to Game Three, the Mets were overlooked and underestimated in their own home park. The Mets didn't put World Series tickets up for sale until they'd clinched a berth. Of course, by that point the Yankees were a win away from advancing to the World Series themselves and their fans could just as easily buy tickets to the games at Shea Stadium.

Which they did. If Shea Stadium didn't feel like a home field for the Yankees by the time first pitch arrived, it certainly didn't provide the home field advantage the Mets might have preferred.

"I thought there were quite a few Yankees fans," Mets reliever Turk Wendell said. "But I don't really care about the Yankees."

Those Mets fans who did get into the building left no doubt about their loyalties. One toted a double-sided sign. One side read, CLEMENS: PINHEAD IN PINSTRIPES, and the other side read, THE HOUSE THAT GEORGE BOUGHT.

One of Steinbrenner's most interesting purchases took the mound for the Yankees in Game Three. After a decade as one of Cuba's best pitchers, Orlando "El Duque" Hernandez boarded a sailboat with seven companions and defected from his native country on Christmas Day 1997.

He took asylum in Costa Rica, which allowed him to negotiate a contract with any team he desired rather than be subject to Major League Baseball's draft. The Yankees provided Hernandez a visa and eventually signed him to a four-year contract worth $6.6 million in March 1998.

Hernandez joined the Yankees in June and immediately lent an unmistakable air of intrigue to a rotation already bursting with a pair of characters in David Cone and David Wells, a homegrown ace in Andy Pettitte, and an international headline-maker in Japan native Hideki Irabu.

Hernandez's agent, Joe Cubas, was soliciting offers to make a movie about his client's life, including a birthday nobody could identify (Hernandez insisted he was 28, though records would later show he was born in October 1965, which made him 32 during his rookie year) and a defection through the shark-infested waters of the Atlantic Ocean, an adventure whose details grew murkier and more mysterious by the day.

"He said he won't answer any questions about his trip," Hernandez's interpreter, Leo Astacio, told *Sports Illustrated* in 1998. "He said he's saving it for the movie."

Hernandez's mystery extended to the mound. The right-hander made up for middling velocity with an arsenal of off-speed pitches—including an "eephus" pitch that couldn't get pulled over on a New York highway—delivered from a variety of arm angles with a high leg kick.

He improvised when the ball was hit, too. In a regular-season Subway Series game against the Mets in 1999, Hernandez leaped to field a comebacker by Rey Ordonez. The ball got wedged in Hernandez's glove, so he threw the entire glove to Tino Martinez for the out.

There was nothing mysterious about Hernandez's success in the playoffs. He entered Game Three 8–0 with a 1.90 ERA in 10 postseason appearances (nine starts). Trying to win a World Series for George Steinbrenner was the most stressful thing most people would endure. Hernandez, of course, had dealt with challenges far more imposing than the expectations of an imperious owner.

"If the sharks didn't distract me, nothing that can happen on a baseball field will," Hernandez told *Sports Illustrated.*

Rick Reed hadn't dealt with sharks, but his path to a Subway Series start was treacherous in its own way. Reed was almost 22 years old when he was drafted in the 24th round of the 1986 draft by the Pittsburgh Pirates out of Marshall University, whose alums had combined to play a grand total of 222 big-league games at the time Reed turned pro. He surged to the majors by 1988 and spent parts of the next six seasons in the bigs.

But Reed, an undersized soft tosser who possessed exquisite command, could not figure out a way to replicate his minor league success. He went 30–16 with a 2.97 ERA for the Pirates' Triple-A affiliate in Buffalo from 1989 to 1991 and posted a 3.09 ERA for the Kansas City Royals' Triple-A affiliate in 1993.

Reed finished the 1994 season with the Cincinnati Reds' Triple-A affiliate, for whom he posted a 4.62 ERA. He turned 30 on August 16, four days after the players went on strike, and was 9–15 with a 4.55 ERA in 57 big-league games.

Reed remained the property of the Reds, and when owners tried to begin the 1995 season with replacement players, he was among the dozens of players throughout the game told to cross the picket line or be released. Reed, who was paying the medical bills for his ill mom, played in replacement games in spring training, which branded him a "scab" once the strike ended and the players returned to work in early April.

He returned to Triple-A, where he went 11–4 with a 3.33 ERA and earned a promotion to the Reds in the midst of the pennant race in July. According to *ESPN The Magazine*, when Reds general manager Jim Bowden informed players of his plans, one stood up and yelled he would not play with a scab.

Reed signed with the Mets following the season and, for the first time since 1987, spent the entire year in the minors despite recording a 3.16 ERA for Triple-A Norfolk. But he found an ally there in Manager Bobby Valentine, who became the big-league manager in August. The next season, Reed won the Mets' fifth starter job and went 13–9 with a 2.89 ERA, the sixth-lowest mark in the NL.

That marked the beginning of a four-season span in which Reed established a reputation as the poor man's Greg Maddux—one of the finest compliments a pitcher could receive in the late 1990s—in going 51–30 with a 3.69 ERA while establishing himself as the Mets' best big-game pitcher.

Reed vaulted the Mets into a tie for the wild card spot by tossing a three-hit shutout on the penultimate day of the 1999 season and threw seven innings of three-hit ball in Game Four of the NL Championship Series, which the Mets won, 3–2, to begin their near comeback from a three-games-to-none deficit. The next night, he was warming in the bullpen in the 15th inning in case the Mets could not score the tie-breaking run in the game Robin Ventura ended with his "Grand Slam Single."

Now, he was pitching the biggest game of his career, and the Mets knew there was nobody they'd rather have on the mound down two games to none.

"He's the guy that you want in the foxhole," said Turk Wendell, his locker room neighbor and close friend. "If you guys are in battle, he's the guy I'd want next to me."

Neither Reed nor Hernandez was known for their strikeout totals, but they were each on record totals early in Game Three. Twelve of the game's first 13 outs—six apiece by each pitcher—were recorded via the strikeout. The record at the time for most strikeouts in a World Series game was 25.

Ventura briefly interrupted the flurry of whiffs with a leadoff homer in the second. The traffic with which Reed and Hernandez were familiar began building in the third, when the Yankees tied the game with two outs as Derek Jeter singled and scored on David Justice's double.

The Yankees went ahead an inning later, when Tino Martinez laced a leadoff single and came home on Paul O'Neill's one-out triple. But the hits by Justice and O'Neill were the only ones Reed allowed in 10 plate appearances with a runner on base.

Initially, Hernandez was even stingier. He kept the Mets hitless in their first eight plate appearances with a runner on base before Todd Zeile tied the game in the sixth when he doubled to bring home Mike Piazza, who led off with a double before Ventura worked a walk. Another walk to Benny Agbayani loaded the bases, after which Hernandez struck out Jay Payton and Mike Bordick and retired Darryl Hamilton—pinch-hitting for Reed—on a grounder.

The Yankees put two runners on in both the seventh, against Wendell and Dennis Cook, and eighth, against Cook and New York City native John Franco, but could not score either time. Hernandez set the Mets down in order in the seventh and struck out Ventura leading off the eighth before a bunch of players who embodied their franchise's past and present teamed up to put the Mets ahead.

Zeile singled up the middle. Two pitches later, Agbayani, who was hitless in his first three at-bats, doubled him home to give the Mets the 3–2 lead.

"El Duque was pitching that game and he was tough," Agbayani says. "I kept on telling Tom Robson, our hitting coach at the time, 'He's coming at me at all kinds of angles, man.' I was like, 'How am I going to hit this guy?' He just said, 'Just [find] one location, put that bat on the ball.' And I did."

The game-winning hit was the second of the postseason for Agbayani, who hit a walk-off homer in Game Three of the NL Division Series against the San Francisco Giants.

Payton singled on the next pitch to send pinch-runner Joe McEwing to third and chase Hernandez. Left-hander Mike Stanton entered for the Yankees, and Valentine, who initially sent up the left-handed-hitting Lenny Harris to pinch-hit for Bordick, answered Joe Torre's move by instead pinch-hitting Bubba Trammell. The trade deadline acquisition singled home McEwing to provide a valuable insurance run.

"We were a bunch of guys just going out there and trying to work together," Agbayani says. "It's like paddling a canoe. Everybody, they were just stroking it the right way. You couldn't ask for anything else better than that. Just had a bunch of guys out there that wanted to win. And when guys didn't do their job the other guys stepped up."

The rally put Franco, the longest-tenured member of the Mets and the son of a New York City sanitation worker who wore his late father's t-shirt under his uniform top, in line for the win. Beleaguered closer Armando Benitez shrugged off a leadoff infield single by Chuck Knoblauch to lock down the save and hand the Yankees their first World Series loss in more than four years.

"It was almost a must-win," Todd Pratt said afterward. "It wasn't an elimination game, but it was as close as you can get with a team that's won 14, 15 World Series games in a row. If we lost tonight, we'd still have confidence, but it would almost be a Mount Everest—four in a row against a team that hasn't lost in four years."

The presence of Agbayani and Payton at the center of the game-winning rally provided a most emphatic underlining of the composition of the 2000 Mets.

Both players were in the organization when Phillips was promoted to general manager, but unlike their fellow holdover teammates, they were far from the majors in 1997.

Payton was a first-round draft pick in 1994 who won batting titles in each of his first two professional seasons before undergoing three operations on his right elbow—including two Tommy John surgeries—between 1995 and 1997 and arthroscopic surgery on his left shoulder in early 1999.

By the time Payton got to spring training in 2000, he was 27 with graying hair. He was also out of options for a team that appeared to have one open roster spot, which led to a battle between Phillips, the general manager who wanted to hang onto a highly touted draft pick, and Valentine, the manager who was loyal to Agbayani after bonding with the overlooked outfielder over the previous several seasons.

Agbayani, a Hawaii native and 30th-round draft pick in 1993, appeared to be what could charitably be dubbed organizational depth after he hit .272 with seven homers in his first 170 games at Single-A ball in 1993 and 1994. Like Reed, Agbayani was one of the minor leaguers nudged to cross a picket line in 1995. And like Reed, he found someone championing his cause in Valentine, who was Agbayani's manager when he hit seven homers and stole 14 bases with Triple-A Norfolk in 1996.

Agbayani became a New York sensation during his big-league debut in 1999, when he hit 10 homers in his first 73 at-bats—the quickest any Mets player has reached 10 homers—and inspired a "Benny and the Mets" parody of Elton John's hit song. But he appeared to be the odd man out as Opening Day 2000 approached. Agbayani demanded a trade, a request Phillips said he would not heed.

The fact the manager liked and fought for Agbayani provided him little solace.

"At least I have somebody in the organization that wants me on the team, right?" Agbayani said in March 2000. "But you know how things in baseball go."

Fortunately for Agbayani, things ended up going his way. The Mets were able to carry Agbayani for their season-opening series against the Chicago Cubs in Japan because fifth starter Glendon Rusch would remain in the minor leagues until his start arrived in mid-April. Agbayani hit the tie-breaking grand slam in the 11th inning of a 5–1 win over the Cubs on March 30.

A little more than a week later, Hamilton hit the disabled list with a toe injury. That saved Agbayani's roster spot, and by the time Hamilton returned in August, he was a reserve, with Agbayani manning left field and Payton patrolling center field.

The potentially awkward battle for one roster spot earlier in the season did not impact the friendship of Agbayani and Payton, who'd become weight-lifting and dinner buddies during their minor league days.

"I knew his swing inside and out, he had that big leg kick," Payton says. "So when things got off for him, I could kind of pick it apart for him. He knew my swing, so we were always helping each other out. Just had a good bond."

By the time the playoffs kicked into gear, Agbayani and Payton were two-thirds of an unlikely starting outfield. Right field was occupied by Timo Perez, the international free agent who signed in March, joined the big-league team in September, and became the leadoff hitter when Derek Bell suffered a season-ending right ankle injury in Game One of the NL Division Series against the San Francisco Giants.

Two games later, Agbayani turned the series in the Mets' favor with his first game-winning hit of the postseason, a walk-off homer in the 13th inning. The one-time replacement player rounded the bases as the song "We Like To Party" shook Shea Stadium. Upon crossing home plate, Payton wrapped him in a giant bear hug and held him tight, two best friends who knew better than anyone else the roundabout path they'd taken to the biggest moments of their lives.

And now Agbayani had recorded the go-ahead hit in the Mets' first World Series win in 14 years—a victory that snapped the Yankees' record World Series winning streak at 14 games.

"I didn't care what anybody said, I didn't care what was going on in the organization," Agbayani says. "This is my time. I'm going to do everything possible to help this ballclub win. I just wanted to do that. I just wanted to prove myself every day I went out there."

The 22nd-round draft pick and former replacement player started the game, the 30th-round draft pick and former replacement player delivered the game-winning hit, and the 40-year-old lifelong New Yorker relying on guts and guile earned the victory. There could be no better summation of the 2000 Mets, a team put together by two vastly different men who nonetheless saw the value in the overlooked and the underrated.

"Bobby did like those sort of guys who had paid a price to get there—the Matt Francos of the world, the Benny Agbayanis of the world, guys like that, he had a connection with," Phillips says. "I think he had an appreciation for what they went through and dealing with the adversity in their careers to get to that point."

"I always thought that the stars wanted to be part of the team and the guys who were at the end of the bench wanted to be part of the team," Valentine says. "And I tried to bring them together."

# CHAPTER 4
# GAME FOUR

**Yankees 3, Mets 2**
**Yankees lead series, three games to one**

**LONG BEFORE JOE** Torre and Bobby Valentine engaged each other in a high-stakes late-inning managerial chess match, long before George Steinbrenner picked up a pail and began bailing water out of the visitor's clubhouse at Shea Stadium, long before Torre put the managerial machinations in motion by pulling Denny Neagle for David Cone, and long before Derek Jeter turned momentum in the Yankees' favor by homering on Bobby Jones's first pitch of Game Four, the question all of America was pondering had to be posed:

Who let the dogs out?

The only guaranteed winner in the 2000 baseball playoffs was the Baha Men. Five of the eight playoff teams hadn't reached the postseason in 1999, and the three holdovers all had serious question marks attached to their World Series candidacy. The dynastic Yankees lost 15 of their final 18 regular-season games. The Mets hadn't done much to indicate they could get over the hump known as the Atlanta Braves, who in turn were beginning to burnish a reputation as regular-season monsters who perennially fell short in October.

Yet whoever got to the World Series, the odds were really good that "Who Let The Dogs Out?" the first one-hit wonder earworm of the century—was going to be the theme/rally song for at least one of the teams. Steve Greenberg, who produced the song for the Baha Men, was so certain the song would become a stadium staple that he began his own record label and hired a marketer to pitch the song to professional sports teams.

But the song took off by accident. Fred Traube, the marketer whom Greenberg hired, brought the song to the Seattle Mariners, who played "Who Let The Dogs Out?" as a joke for catcher Joe Oliver. Traube, speaking to *Sports Illustrated* in 2015, said the Mariners used it as Oliver's walk-up song because he was ". . . a country-western catcher, a square white guy" and the team wanted ". . . to break his balls" by blasting it.

Except a more decorated teammate ended up liking the song, too.

"Alex Rodriguez liked it so much, he stole the song for himself," Traube said of the future Yankees third baseman and source of Reggie Jackson-esque tabloid fodder.

Rodriguez's stamp of approval helped Greenberg realize his goal. By the time the playoffs started, "Who Let The Dogs Out?" was inescapable on the radio, and six of the teams still playing baseball were to some degree using the song as a rallying cry, including the normally stodgy Yankees.

But no one played it as loud or as often or embraced the song as tightly as the Mets. Closer Armando Benitez used it as his entrance music and became friends with the Baha Men's band members. New York's most popular radio station, Z100, produced a parody titled "Who Let The Mets Out?"

The real song played after Mets wins and in the clubhouse. During

Game Five of the NL Championship Series, "Who Let The Dogs Out?" blasted after Todd Zeile's bases-clearing double in the fourth inning and again as the Mets celebrated their pennant-clinching victory.

A few days later, Zeile appeared on *Good Morning America* with the Baha Men and watched with his son as the band performed its signature hit.

"It was a little bit odd because I don't think they really cared about baseball or anything like that," Zeile says. "It was a thing, for sure, and it became sort of our calling card at the end of that season."

The Baha Men completed their unusual ascension into the American zeitgeist before Game Four, when they performed their hit song in front of the Mets dugout prior to the first pitch, after Sheryl Crow's rendition of "The Star-Spangled Banner."

It was, as far as anyone could tell, the first time anyone went to a baseball game and watched a concert break out. (Those who wanted to see a full Baha Men set could have done so the next night, when the band played a show at a theater on Long Island.)

It was also the perfect embodiment of the differences between New York's baseball teams.

For the Mets, followed by a fan base conditioned to treat each victorious moment with unbridled joy because they never knew when another would arrive, giddily attaching themselves to a one-hit wonder was the appropriate thing to do, especially after a Game Three win that symbolized how their scrappy, collective nature seemed to have turned the momentum in their favor.

"Because of the fact that we were in every game, [each game] was a one-run differential, after we won Game Three, I think we felt like, hey, we can beat them again here at home," Zeile says. "We'll have one more here and then we can go back up on them. I think we felt very confident at that point, even down 2–1, that this was ours to win now. And I think a lot of people believed that, too."

For the Yankees—the regal team represented in victory by Frank Sinatra's timeless "New York, New York"—and their fans, the sight of a flavor-of-the-month performing at a World Series game was one to be greeted with a lot of bewilderment and maybe just a little condescension.

"When we came here, they had that group playing," Yankees utilityman Jose Vizcaino says. "We were laughing. We were enjoying it, because in that moment, that was the song that everybody would listen to. We knew that was a big thing.

"I think that was more motivation for us to beat them."

After the Baha Men's performance, Mets staffers scurried around to clear the area in front of the home dugout. Eventually, Mets starter Bobby Jones began warming up to the strains of Metallica's "For Whom The Bell Tolls."

And then the player who most embodied the differences between the two teams stepped to the plate and, with one swing, permanently swung the Subway Series momentum back in the Yankees' favor.

***

It only seemed like the Yankees were comprised of players who had spent their careers living a charmed existence. Of the 10 players who were a part of all four World Series-winning teams, four—David Cone, Tino Martinez, Jeff Nelson, and Paul O'Neill—reached the bigs with other organizations.

Most of the six homegrown players to earn four rings between 1996 and 2000 all endured their share of challenges before becoming integral parts of the dynasty. Mariano Rivera, signed for $2,500 in 1990, underwent right elbow surgery in 1992 and posted a 5.51 ERA as a 25-year-old rookie in 1995. Jorge Posada, selected in the 24th round of the 1990 draft as a second baseman, converted to catcher in the low minors and didn't become a full-time player until 2000, the season in which he turned 28 years old. Ramiro Mendoza, who signed with the Yankees in 1991, shuffled between the rotation and the bullpen, posted a 4.10 ERA in pinstripes, and wasn't on the postseason roster in 1996 or 2000.

Bernie Williams, who signed with the organization in 1985, and Andy Pettitte, who was selected out of high school in the 22nd round of the 1990 draft and signed the following spring after a season at junior college, both had their off-field gentleness mistaken for a lack of on-field aggression. As a rookie, the then-bespectacled Williams was bullied by veteran teammates, who dubbed him "Bambi." Fiery owner George Steinbrenner had to be talked out of trading both Williams and Pettitte, and he needed a last-second plea by Williams to retain the center fielder as a free agent following the 1998 season.

And then there was Derek Jeter, whose ascension was not without turbulence. But he seemed destined for stardom from the moment he landed in the Yankees' laps in the 1992 draft.

As a senior at Kalamazoo Central High School in Michigan, Jeter hit .508 with one strikeout in 59 at-bats and won National Player of the Year honors from the American Baseball Coaches Association. Even accounting for his commitment to the University of Michigan, there was little doubt he was one of the best players, if not the best, in the draft.

Yet the five teams selecting ahead of the Yankees all passed on Jeter. The Houston Astros, picking first, believed Jeter would want a $1 million signing bonus to turn pro and selected Cal State-Fullerton infielder Phil Nevin, who signed for $700,000. The Astros made the pick over the objections of Hal Newhouser, their Michigan-based scout who often drove several hours one way to watch Jeter's high school games. Newhouser was so upset by the Astros' choice that he resigned.

The next four teams—the Cleveland Indians, Montreal Expos, Baltimore Orioles, and Cincinnati Reds—all picked collegians. Nevin, second overall pick Paul Shuey, fourth pick Jeffrey Hammonds, and fifth pick Chad Mottola combined to appear in 2,343 big league games, 404 fewer than Jeter. The Expos' pick, B.J. Wallace, made 48 appearances as a professional, eight above the Single-A level.

When the Yankees picked Jeter, it set into motion a success story that would have sounded too hokey if it'd been penned by an aspiring scriptwriter. Jeter, who was born in New Jersey before moving to

Michigan with his family at four years old, wrote an essay in eighth grade in which he detailed his plan to grow up to become the Yankees' shortstop. As a junior in high school, Jeter took a British literature class in which one of the assignments was to design a coat of arms. Jeter's was that of a baseball player swinging a bat and wearing a Yankees uniform.

Jeter signed with the Yankees for $800,000 and batted .210 with 21 errors in his first 58 professional games in 1992. The next season, he committed 56 errors while playing for Single-A Greensboro. Jeter would later say he'd often cry himself to sleep and that he'd heard rumblings the Yankees were considering a position switch.

A decade earlier, Jeter might have been shifted to the outfield or traded for someone George Steinbrenner believed could immediately help the Yankees. But general manager Gene Michael was running the franchise without interference from the suspended Steinbrenner. And the longtime Yankees executive believed Jeter would thrive as a shortstop in the bigs.

"Jeter had made like 40-some errors, but he tells me this guy is going to be an All-Star shortstop," then-Yankees manager Buck Showalter told reporters after Michael's death in 2017. "He said he's got a little footwork issue.

"How do you project those things and stand by them?"

Michael was right. Struggles that would swallow other players were ankle-high hurdles easily cleared by Jeter, who cut his errors to 25 in 1994 while batting .344 with five homers, 68 RBIs, and 50 stolen bases between three minor league levels. At least three publications—including *Baseball America*—named him the minor league player of the year.

Jeter's most impressive stat was his winning percentage. The teams he played for went 87–53 (a .621 winning percentage) with him on the roster and 138–137 (a .502 winning percentage) without him.

In every way, Jeter ended the 1994 season as the most promising prospect in the game. He impressed teammates and management alike with his work ethic as well as his leadership skills and mature demeanor.

As children, Derek and his younger sister, Sharlee, signed contracts with their parents spelling out the expectations for the upcoming school year. There was never a need for the Yankees' minor league staff to spend a fitful night worrying where Jeter was or what he was doing.

Jeter made his big-league debut in 1995, when he batted .250 in 15 games and watched from the bench as the Yankees fell to the Seattle Mariners in a five-game AL Division Series. He was penciled in as the starter at shortstop in 1996, but Steinbrenner expressed his impatience when Jeter struggled both at the plate and in the field during spring training. Steinbrenner ordered the front office to pursue a trade for a proven veteran at the position.

The Mariners were willing to deal their backup shortstop, Felix Fermin, to the Yankees for a then-little known swingman, Mariano Rivera. Steinbrenner convened his baseball people to discuss the choice: make the trade or stick with Jeter?

First-year Manager Joe Torre and his staff supported Jeter, as did Assistant General Manager Brian Cashman. But Steinbrenner wasn't swayed until Michael, the former Yankees shortstop turned general manager now turned scout, implored Steinbrenner to give Jeter a shot throughout the first half of the season. Steinbrenner agreed, and the trade offer was taken off the table.

Jeter became the first rookie to start at shortstop for the Yankees in more than 30 years. Batting ninth against the Cleveland Indians, Jeter homered in his second at-bat and made a terrific back-to-the-plate catch to rob Omar Vizquel of an RBI hit in the seventh inning of the Yankees' 7–1 win.

It was the first of the innumerable times Jeter would display an almost supernatural ability to be in the right place at the right time and to save his biggest plays for the biggest moments. After hitting .314 with 10 homers and 78 RBIs in 157 games—a performance that would earn him unanimous American League Rookie of the Year honors—for the AL East champion Yankees, Jeter opened the playoffs by hitting .412 in a four-game win over the Texas Rangers in the AL Division Series.

But his legend really began to build in the eighth inning of Game One of the AL Championship Series against the Orioles, when, with the Yankees down 4–3 and five outs away from defeat, Jeter lofted a fly ball to deep right field. The Orioles' Tony Tarasco settled at the wall, put his glove up . . . and had the ball grabbed out of the air by 12-year-old fan Jeffrey Maier.

Tarasco immediately began pointing skyward, indicating Maier interfered with his attempt to catch the ball and that Jeter should have been called out due to fan interference. But right-field umpire Rich Garcia signaled home run.

Tarasco charged Garcia, gesturing wildly, getting into Garcia's face and making contact with the umpire. Benitez and manager Davey Johnson were among those who raced out to right field to argue with Tarasco, but it was to no avail. The home run stood, and Jeter was credited with the game-tying homer—his third hit in four at-bats out of the no. 9 spot in the order.

Jeter added a single in the 10th inning before Williams homered leading off the 11th to give the Yankees a 5–4 victory. The Yankees went on to win the ALCS in five games and won their first World Series in 18 years by beating the Atlanta Braves in six games. Jeter finished the playoffs with a .361 average.

From 1996 to 2000, Jeter batted .323 in the regular season while emerging as the unquestioned leader of a dynastic team that was loaded with 30-something veterans. He also became the Joe DiMaggio of his generation, dating a bevy of Hollywood starlets, collecting armfuls worth of endorsements, and turning into a staple of the gossip pages without ever letting the nightlife impact his on-field performance.

Jeter raised his game to an even higher level during the playoffs. In 45 postseason games from 1996 to 1999, he batted .326 and produced a 17-game hitting streak, tied for the longest postseason hitting streak of all time.

"I always describe Jeter with the benefit of hindsight—kind of knew it along the way—but he just [had] the best stay-in-the-present kind of mentality of a player, the best I've ever seen," David Cone says. "Call it a turn-the-page guy. 5-for-5 or 0-for-5 the day before, it doesn't matter. Tomorrow doesn't really matter. It's right here, right now."

The Yankees, in an uncomfortable and unfamiliar position, needed someone with that mentality to set the tone for Game Four of the World Series. The loss to the Mets the night before snapped a 14-game World Series winning streak that dated back to 1996, when the Yankees fell behind the Braves two games to none and were decided underdogs heading back to Atlanta.

Four years later, the Yankees were the favorites for whom losing was not an option.

"We had gone through a pretty good streak," Joe Torre says. "We never had to face the losing. But losing, especially in postseason, is so dramatic, because of the momentum shift."

Across the field, the Mets felt the momentum had turned their way. The Yankees were on their turf—watching the Mets' band perform a decidedly Mets song, to boot—and the Mets believed they'd not only head back across the Triborough Bridge for a Game Six three nights later, but that they'd do so with the series lead.

The Mets believed it right up until 8:31 p.m., when, 13 minutes after the first pitch was scheduled to be thrown, Jeter finally stepped into the batter's box. He was batting leadoff for the first time since Game Four of the ALDS and for what would be the only time in the World Series.

At 8:31 p.m., Jones threw his first pitch.

And at 8:31 p.m., with flash bulbs popping throughout Shea Stadium, Jeter swung and hit a home run to left field.

The reaction was swift and visceral on both sides.

"I was sitting right there on the little stool in the on-deck circle," Mets reliever Turk Wendell says. "And I just said, 'Aww shit.'"

"He was not known as a home run hitter," former Mets media relations director Jay Horwitz says. "He hits the home run the first pitch. It was a portend of not good things to happen."

"I do remember it being a gut punch, because as Derek goes, they go," Zeile says. "He's just always so productive in big moments. And that was a way to start it off. We had a little bit of momentum from Game Three. We felt like . . ."

Zeile snapped his fingers.

"They snagged it from us immediately."

The Mets spent 27 outs and 149 pitches grinding out a Game Three victory in their sum-is-better-than-the-parts style, and all it took was one swing of the bat by the most decorated of the seven dynasty-era players who would end up with a plaque in Monument Park to turn the momentum back in the Yankees' favor.

"It gave our whole bench a lift," Cone says. "Collectively, everybody jumped out of their seat on the bench."

"Jeter does what he does, it's a big deal, no question about it," Scott Brosius says. "It injects energy and you love to see something on the board right away."

"We lost [Game Three] and we come back and I sort of juggle the lineup a little bit, had Derek lead off, and he hits the first-pitch home run," Torre says. "It was like, just sort of exhale—not that you knew you were going to win, but it sort of turned momentum a little bit to our side."

Jeter's leadoff homer set the tone for an urgently managed swing game that would turn into a chess match between Torre and Bobby Valentine, whose complicated history with each other and similar yet divergent paths to managing in New York lent an additional layer of intrigue to an already fascinating World Series.

After a Hall of Fame-caliber career in which he won the NL MVP award in 1971 and made nine All-Star teams, Torre made a seamless transition to managing in 1977, when he spent a few weeks as the Mets' player-manager before retiring as a player to focus fully on his new career.

Torre was still living in both worlds during the most seismic day in team history—June 15, when the Mets made three trades and acquired seven players. The biggest deal sent "The Franchise," disgruntled ace Tom Seaver, to the Cincinnati Reds.

Two days later, one of the players the Mets acquired for Seaver, pitcher Pat Zachry, made his debut for his new team. In the sixth inning, Torre pinch-hit for Zachry with another newcomer, Bobby Valentine. The utilityman, who had been acquired from the San Diego Padres in exchange for slugger Dave Kingman, drew a walk.

The next time the pitcher's spot came up, Torre inserted himself as pinch-hitter. Torre, who was a month away from his 37th birthday, recorded a flyout in the final plate appearance of his big-league career.

Despite playing infrequently, Valentine quickly became a valued veteran leader for Torre, who was presiding over a rebuilding team in the midst of the first of four straight 90-loss seasons. But Valentine, still battling the effects of the career-altering leg injury he suffered in 1973, made just 188 plate appearances in 1978 and lost out on the battle for the final roster spot late in spring training in 1979. A furious Valentine called a press conference to declare he'd been led to believe he'd made the team and that being released by a last-place team so close to Opening Day could end his career.

Valentine did latch on with the Seattle Mariners, for whom he played the 1979 season before retiring and beginning his coaching career with the Mets. He also came to understand Torre wasn't wrong in the spring of 1979.

"When he first released me I took it personally," Valentine says. "And when I had time to look back at it, I realized it was a good decision, because I couldn't play anymore."

Torre was fired by the Mets following the 1981 strike season and was almost immediately named the manager of another one of his former teams, the Atlanta Braves. With Torre at the helm, the Braves won their first 13 games—the longest season-opening winning streak in baseball history—and went on to win the NL West. But Torre's first trip to the playoffs was a brief one, as the St. Louis Cardinals swept in three games.

Torre lasted two more seasons with the Braves before being fired and becoming a broadcaster with the California Angels prior to the

1985 season—the same season in which the Texas Rangers, one of the Angels' AL West rivals, fired manager Doug Rader and replaced him with Valentine, who'd opened the season as the manager of the Mets' Triple-A affiliate.

Torre returned to the dugout on August 1, 1990, when his third former team, the St. Louis Cardinals, hired him to replace future Hall of Famer Whitey Herzog. But the Cardinals finished higher than third just once and never made the playoffs under Torre before he was fired in June 1995.

At the time, Torre was almost 55 years old and more than 100 games under .500 (894-1,003) as a big-league manager. He'd played or managed in more games (4,106) without reaching the World Series than anyone in baseball history. He figured his managerial days were over.

So Torre was as surprised as anyone when he was asked to interview for the Yankees' job in October. While the position remained one of the crown jewels in sports, the franchise appeared to be returning to its old ways under a reinstated and reinvigorated George Steinbrenner. Following a five-game AL Division Series loss to the Mariners, General Manager Gene Michael, who had rebuilt the farm system in Steinbrenner's absence, quit. Manager Buck Showalter, a Yankees lifer, was not offered a new contract.

Still, one more chance to manage—in his hometown, no less—was impossible to resist for Torre. On November 2, 1995, he signed a two-year deal and was introduced as the Yankees' newest manager.

"I always felt it was a bonus opportunity for me," Torre says. "Because the three teams I played for, I managed. And then that was gone because they all fired me."

The reception Torre received was decidedly skeptical—the *New York Daily News* welcomed the Big Apple native back home with a back-page headline reading CLUELESS JOE—and familiar.

When the Yankees hired 58-year-old Casey Stengel in 1948, they were bringing aboard a manager whose previous two teams—the

Brooklyn Dodgers and Boston Bees/Braves—went a combined 581–742 and never finished higher than fifth in the National League.

"I know writers and I kept hearing a hum from writers in the room," Stengel told author Roger Kahn in *The Era*. "And the writers were looking at me, damn near sixty years old, and they're saying, in this hum: 'That old bum managed nine years before in the major leagues and he never once got out of the second division.'"

Stengel had at least made it to three World Series as a player. Shortly after being hired by the Yankees, Torre admitted he was driven by getting to a World Series and plagued by what-ifs regarding his most recent near miss. He told *Newsday*'s Marty Noble the Mets offered to trade him to the contending Yankees in 1976, the season before he took over as manager.

"I said I didn't want to go if it was going to cost me a chance to manage in the future," Torre said. "So I could regret my decision because it cost me a chance to get into the World Series. But if I'd said yes, I might never have managed."

As it turned out, he'd get to the World Series with the Yankees—over and over and over and over and over again.

Valentine was as driven as Torre to parlay an opportunity to manage an area baseball team into the World Series trip he'd yearned to make the previous several decades. Unlike Torre, though, Valentine was left to wonder in the mid-'90s if he'd even get a second chance.

Even as he climbed the professional ladder faster than Torre—he became the Rangers' manager two days after his 35th birthday in 1985—Valentine knew he was not nearly as accepted as most of his peers. His close friendship with polarizing Los Angeles Dodgers manager Tommy Lasorda—who declared more than once he'd like Valentine to eventually replace him as skipper—was one factor in his relative ostracism, as was the fact Valentine had interests that extended well beyond the diamond.

"I didn't hunt and fish and play golf," Valentine says. "People didn't like that I did different things."

If Torre was following Stengel's footsteps in turning an otherwise ordinary managerial career into a Hall of Fame one upon taking the reins of the Yankees, Valentine was Stengel-esque in his ability to successfully dabble in a variety of industries and engage fans at a uniquely human level.

Stengel invested in Texas oil fields during his playing days and spent the year between managing the Yankees and Mets as an executive at a bank owned by his wife's family. Valentine not only starred in various sports during his teenage years, he also found the time to perform as the lead in the school play and turn himself into a national champion ballroom dancer—and a champion pancake eater.

Immediately after his playing days ended, Valentine opened a restaurant in his hometown of Stamford, where he said he invented the wrap. (The toaster didn't work, so Valentine rolled what would have been his club sandwich into a tortilla.)

Valentine opened another restaurant in Texas shortly after he became the manager of the Rangers and did the same at a Holiday Inn blocks away from Shea Stadium after being named the Mets' manager. Whether at his restaurants or at the ballpark, Valentine was about selling the team for whom he was employed.

"That's the other thing that I think that Lasorda did, and that I did and that the other managers refused to do, and that was embrace the fandom, to try to make them part of what we were doing, rather than working harder to keep them in the dark on what we were doing," Valentine says. "Other than maybe Casey and Billy [Martin] and Tommy, I'm not sure if anybody else ever put the time in that it takes to embrace and cultivate a fandom."

Valentine brimmed with self-confidence in all his endeavors and was not afraid to suggest new ways to approach baseball, a game rooted in tradition. Long before he was exiled from Japan despite finding success with his unique approach to training, Valentine found himself mocked with the Rangers for putting an emphasis on getting the ball into the air and instituting pitch limits for his starting pitchers.

The Rangers ranked eighth in the majors in homers from 1986 through 1991, Valentine's six full seasons as manager. In 1991, the Rangers had just nine complete games, third-fewest in the American League, while Hall of Fame-bound starting pitcher Nolan Ryan, who threw the fifth-most innings (5,386) of all-time, averaged 105 pitches per game.

"I was always the renegade," Valentine says. "I was the one that was talking about swinging up in the '80s. I was the one that was not afraid to take Nolan Ryan out of the game even though he was the greatest starting pitcher that there was. I did different things the fraternity never liked. They wanted to beat down that protruding nail, you know?"

While Torre was hired to manage the Braves fewer than three weeks after being fired by the Mets, Valentine traveled around the world before getting another opportunity to manage in the bigs. Valentine sandwiched a pair of stints managing the Mets' Triple-A affiliate around his one season in Japan with Chiba Lotte in 1995.

When he was named the Mets' manager on August 26, 1996, Valentine admitted he'd been a little too headstrong and arrogant as a manager in his mid-30s and that he was looking forward to displaying a gentler touch in his second go-round.

Still, his reputation preceded him. The day after Valentine was hired, Noble wrote that in 1991, during Valentine's tenure with the Rangers, an opponent declared a Valentine-managed team would ". . . have to be 10 games better than all the others to win by five games, because we'll do whatever we can to beat him."

That included excluding Valentine from the managerial equivalent of "discovery"—the exchange of information between lawyers in a trial.

"One of the only regrets that I have about that was that I never was the benefactor of information from other managers," Valentine says. "And I know that there were times when teams would leave Arlington and they'd leave notes on the desk for the incoming manager, about what to look out for to beat me. I never enjoyed that fruit."

No wonder, then, that his players sensed Valentine enjoyed his clashes with the most decorated members of the managerial fraternity.

"I know that I always felt like Bobby was in the chess match with the opposing manager, especially if your last name was Torre or [Tony] LaRussa, [Bobby] Cox, those guys, [Jim] Leyland, whatever," Todd Zeile says. "I always felt like there was a little bit more thought and there was just a little more going into the moves in those games."

There was no better opportunity for Valentine to match wits with the establishment than in the Subway Series. And while Torre and Valentine had mended their relationship in the two-plus decades between their time together with the Mets—their disagreement regarding Roger Clemens's intent when beaning Mike Piazza aside—their showdown was underlined by their vastly different approaches in the dugout and clubhouse.

Torre, a decade older than Valentine, was stoic and stern-faced, rarely moving from his seat in the dugout. He engaged with players regarding the makeup of the lineups and made them feel a part of the decision-making process.

"My first playoff game with the Yankees, against Texas, we were facing [John] Burkett," Torre says. "And [Darryl] Strawberry and Big Daddy, Cecil [Fielder]—I couldn't play both of them. Strawberry came into the clubhouse first. I said, 'Straw, come on in here, I've got to ask you a question.' He said, 'What can I do for you?' I said, 'I'm not sure who to DH, you or Big Daddy.' And he says 'Have Big Daddy DH, I can handle sitting on the bench better.'

"I didn't listen to him. I played him. He went 0-for-4."

Valentine, perched atop the top step of the dugout, was active and demonstrative, often appearing as if his mood swung with each pitch. Nobody was spared from his almost daily lineup tinkering, and he didn't often consult with the players. During a losing streak that threatened to knock the Mets out of the wild card spot in late September 1999, Valentine dropped usual no. 2 hitter Edgardo Alfonzo into the sixth spot, which Alfonzo learned when he walked into the locker room and saw the lineup posted on the wall.

The next September, after the Mets' NL East title hopes were all but extinguished with back-to-back losses to the Atlanta Braves, Valentine called a team meeting in which he tore into his players and saved his most profane invective for the Mets' best player—MVP candidate Mike Piazza.

Wrote Piazza in his autobiography, *Long Shot*: "Then, before it broke up, he said something to the effect of 'Mike, I don't know if you're tired or if you don't give a fuck, but if you don't want to be in there, let me know.'"

In their own different ways, though, Torre and Valentine were doing the same thing: shielding their players and shouldering the pressure. Torre absorbed the most impatient rants from George Steinbrenner, and the fatherly tone he struck in conversations about the lineup and other topics was his way of assuring the Yankees that Steinbrenner's panicked nature wasn't trickling down to the locker room, which was a feat none of his predecessors could master.

"He always was calm," Yankees reliever Jeff Nelson says. "I mean, he would let you know if you weren't doing well and question some of your pitches or what you're doing in your at-bats. But he was a guy that—I guess when you have managers and a coaching staff that doesn't panic, it just carries over to the rest of the clubhouse. And when he believes in you, just like in '96, when we were down 0–2 going into the [World Series games at the] Braves? Nothing. There was no panic whatsoever."

And if Valentine made himself the target of scorn inside and outside his locker room (after the Braves eliminated the Mets on the final day of the 1998 season, superstar third baseman Chipper Jones said, "We knocked 'Top Step' off the top step") or invited negative attention? That was less scorn and negative attention that would be bestowed upon the players, who could focus on their jobs.

When general manager Steve Phillips fired three of Valentine's coaches after the Mets started 27–28 in 1999, Valentine said he should be fired if the Mets didn't play much better over the next 55 games—a span in which they went 40–15. When the Mets endured a seven-game losing streak in the final week of the season, Valentine said he shouldn't be retained if the Mets missed the playoffs. They earned the wild card berth and made the NL Championship Series.

The playoff appearance in 1999 validated Valentine, who entered that season having managed more games in the divisional play era without making the postseason than any other skipper. Now he was in the World Series for the first time with a chance to battle the best, most universally respected manager in the game—someone who, like Valentine, was going to manage Game Four like it represented his first chance at a ring and not his fourth.

***

Up two games to one, the Yankees weren't officially in must-win mode. But the longer the series went, the more difficult the task would become for a team that stumbled into October, overcame deficits in its first two playoff series, and was loaded with aging players who'd played dozens upon dozens of playoff games the previous five seasons.

The faster the Yankees could put a stranglehold on the series, the better. And that wasn't going to happen if the Mets won Game Four and turned the World Series into a best-of-three affair.

"You know, 3-to-1's a whole lot better than 2-to-2," Torre says.

To get to a 3–1 series lead, Torre would rely on his most trusted lieutenants, even if it meant fracturing his relationship with one of the Yankees' newest players.

The Yankees scored single runs in the second and third to expand their lead to 3–0. Paul O'Neill tripled with one out in the second. Already recognizing the value of runs, Valentine intentionally walked Jorge Posada to set up a double play. But Scott Brosius lofted a sacrifice fly.

In the third inning, Jeter struck again, this time with a leadoff triple. Luis Sojo followed with an RBI groundout.

The Mets struck back in the bottom of the third, when Timo Perez hit a leadoff single against Denny Neagle and Piazza crushed a two-run homer. The blast improved Piazza's career average against Neagle to a robust .379 and set Torre's mind racing.

"You make up your mind that a one-run lead's enough, because that's the kind of bullpen I trusted," Torre says. "I'm sitting next to 'Zim' [bench coach Don Zimmer] and I said, 'I can't let Neagle pitch to Piazza again, OK?'"

Neagle retired seven of the next eight batters he faced, including Perez and Edgardo Alfonzo on two pitches apiece to open the fifth. The left-hander was one out away from qualifying for a win and had thrown just 73 pitches.

Today, managers (with "input" from the general managers with whom they "collaborate") regularly pull starters with a low pitch count before they can complete five innings and qualify for a victory. In 2000, though, it was almost unheard of, even in a World Series game, for a manager to not allow his starter to complete five innings with the lead.

But Torre did not trust Neagle, who posted a 5.81 ERA in 16 regular-season appearances following his acquisition from the Cincinnati Reds in July, the way he trusted literally everyone else in his lineup that night. And so Torre, in a move that stunned just about everyone in the park—especially Neagle—and anyone else watching or listening to the game, headed to the mound and signaled for a right-hander.

The manager who evoked memories of Casey Stengel upon his unpopular hiring was once again taking a page from a book originally authored by "The Old Perfessor." In Game Three of Stengel's first World Series with the Yankees in 1949, he pulled starter Tommy Byrne for Joe Page with two outs in the fourth inning and the Yankees and Brooklyn Dodgers knotted at 1–1. Wrote Roger Kahn in *The Era*:

"But here Stengel saw—he was phenomenal at this perception—the ballgame at an absolutely critical point. What might happen in the seventh or eighth inning wouldn't matter if the Yankees lost the ballgame in the fourth."

More than half a century later, Neagle, his face etched in equal parts surprise and disgust, handed Torre the ball and stalked into the dugout, grimacing occasionally. After exchanging fist bumps with a handful of teammates, Neagle disappeared into the tunnel leading into the clubhouse.

"I went out to get him, he thought I was just going out to talk to him," Torre said in September 2019. "He hasn't said a word to me since that day."

Torre's biggest surprise wasn't pulling Neagle, but replacing him with David Cone.

"I knew Piazza was the guy that was my matchup, Torre had told me to be ready for Mike," Cone says. "I didn't think it would be two outs with nobody on in the fifth inning."

The beloved right-hander, who was the ace of the Mets from 1988 until his trade to the Toronto Blue Jays in 1992, was acquired by the Yankees in 1995, served as the unofficial team spokesman during the dynasty era, and cemented his spot in franchise lore by throwing a perfect game on July 18, 1999.

But the 2000 season seemed to be the flip side of a Faustian bargain for Cone, who went 4–14 with a 6.91 ERA—the second-highest single-season ERA posted this century by a pitcher with at least 150 innings pitched. Not surprisingly, Cone was relegated to the bullpen for the playoffs. He made just one appearance in the first two rounds and tossed a scoreless inning in a mop-up appearance in Game Five of the AL Championship Series.

"I had a different role, clearly," Cone says. "I was a little punchy because I was used to being in the middle of things and I was marginalized at that point, to a certain extent."

He was coming back from exile for the biggest at-bat of the series. While Torre loved Cone's guts and big-game experience—Cone's win in Atlanta in Game Three of the 1996 World Series jump-started the Yankees' comeback from a two-games-to-none deficit and became one of the defining moments of the championship run—he also liked the matchup of Cone, an unpredictable soft tosser flinging sliders and 85 mph fastballs from a variety of arm angles, against the powerful Piazza.

"Denny had good stuff that night," Torre says. "He was fastball-changeup. And he threw harder than David. But he didn't have as many things to look for for a hitter."

Cone jogged out of the bullpen at 10:14 p.m., initially to a surprised silence and then to a mixture of boos and cheers. The 37-year-old feared he had only two chances to get away with throwing a strike to Piazza, who usually took the first pitch of every at-bat. But Cone's first offering, a fastball, missed.

"I was like, man, that was my chance to get a strike," Cone says.

The wily veteran took a deep breath and hoped Piazza would be extra patient with the 1–0 count. Cone threw another 85 mph fastball, this one right down the middle. Piazza took it for strike one.

Cone's third pitch was a slider, which Piazza swung through for strike two. Cone threw another slider, and Piazza, possibly sensing fastball, lunged across the plate a split-second late and fouled off the pitch.

Jorge Posada, the catcher and another core member of the dynasty, then signaled for a fastball, perhaps figuring Piazza didn't think Cone would challenge him with another pedestrian fastball.

Piazza popped out to second for the third out. It was the final pitch Cone would throw for the Yankees.

"I'm not sure if he was on it or missed," Cone says. "It worked, for whatever reason. I think it probably did surprise him that I would try that pitch. I was just following Posada's lead at that point."

Across the field, Valentine admired the chutzpah of Torre, who had just made his biggest move of the game with 13 outs left to go.

"The only thing that it said at the bottom of the managers' Bill of Rights was don't ever be surprised," Valentine says. "The only time I was surprised was the David Cone move. I was praying against it, especially because it was the fifth inning and [back] then, wins were important.

"And because Denny wasn't one of his boys and he was just a rent-a-arm that he was able to kind of shit on. Joe wouldn't have ever done that with [Andy] Pettitte. Never would have done that with 'Duque'

[Orlando Hernandez]. But he was allowed to do it there and that situation presented itself and he took advantage of it."

As for Neagle never talking to Torre again?

"That's the one thing that I learned about the postseason: you're there to win games not friends," Torre says. "It was just something I felt, because Piazza was so good."

The Yankees had just gotten out of one mess. Inside the visiting clubhouse at Shea Stadium, George Steinbrenner was about to discover another.

***

Even before he picked up a pail to try and scoop out the water climbing to his knees, Steinbrenner wasn't a fan of the Yankees' accommodations at Shea Stadium. Like most visiting clubhouses in facilities constructed in the 1960s or earlier, it was cramped. The surroundings seemed especially small to the Yankees, who were used to luxurious digs across town and had their space on the road further minimized by a large traveling corps of media—a corps that was exponentially larger in the World Series.

In particular, Steinbrenner was annoyed by the seating choices presented to the Yankees. The couches and lounge chairs were not nearly as cushy as the ones the Yankees resided upon at home. And the chairs at their lockers weren't chairs at all.

"They had stools," Yankees director of media relations Rick Cerrone says. "And [Steinbrenner] says, 'This is not going to cut it.'"

Steinbrenner ordered the Yankees' equipment manager, Rob Cucuzza, to transport the furniture and locker chairs from Yankee Stadium. And so everything was loaded into a truck and transported to Shea Stadium. Of course, taking the Yankees' bigger furniture and chairs and placing them inside the tiny visitor's locker room across town . . .

"Made the thing a little smaller," Cerrone says.

Was it Steinbrenner just trying to tweak the Mets by shaming them about the condition of the visiting locker room? Maybe. But this was also the owner who'd catered food during the infamous split-stadium doubleheader earlier in the year. If there was an advantage to be gleaned from maximizing the comfort of his players, Steinbrenner would do his best to exploit it.

"He thought [bringing in furniture] would give us a psychological advantage," Cone told the *New York Post* shortly after Steinbrenner's death in 2010. "And we ended up winning two out of three games."

Plus, if Steinbrenner was going to watch the games from inside the clubhouse, he wanted to be comfortable. As the highest-profile owner in sports, Steinbrenner was regularly captured by the cameras during playoff telecasts. But with the Subway Series stressing him out more than any of his seven previous World Series, it was too much to ask Steinbrenner to conceal his feelings in a seat near the field for three straight nights.

"He was in the clubhouse, which I thought, boy, that puts a lot of pressure on the team," Cerrone says. "You go in there to use the bathroom, go get a drink of water, and that's who was sitting there."

With Steinbrenner behind closed doors, Cone decided to have some fun with the owner. There were cable wires along the floor in the visiting clubhouse in preparation for post-game locker room coverage. Cone told Steinbrenner the cables were installed by the Mets, who were trying to spy on the Yankees. Steinbrenner got on his hands and knees and began pulling at the wires until he realized Cone was playing a practical joke.

"That whole scene was unreal with George," Cone says. "He was around during the season, but not a lot. And then in the postseason, he was there 24/7. Moving furniture over from Yankee Stadium, rearranging the furniture at Shea Stadium, getting there before everybody, sitting on the couch the whole pregame session. During the games—yelling at the TV, at the umpires, at the calls at the game, like a fan. It was really remarkable to see that [transformation] take place.

"So it was ripe for a practical joke. It was ripe for somebody that had the guts to do it."

But Cone couldn't take credit for the flood, though some conspiracy theorists may still believe its cause wasn't as simple as the official explanation made it: a water pipe running above the trainers room in the visiting clubhouse burst and drenched the locker room in water that ran two feet deep.

"I was in there when it happened," Jeff Nelson said afterward. "All of a sudden, the massage room and the weight area and the hot tub area—it was like Niagara Falls. It was all of a sudden, the ceiling collapsed.

"There was water everywhere—this green, gunky water."

The New York City Fire Department was called to the scene—and so were some other people whose job description did not usually call for stepping into a flooded fire hazard.

"I got a call in the press box," Cerrone says. "'Mr. Steinbrenner wants you in the clubhouse immediately.'"

Steinbrenner was among the occupants in the room when the pipe burst. The then-69-year-old, who'd once been a champion hurdler and a football coach, picked up buckets and began trying to bail the water.

In addition to asking Cerrone for assistance once he arrived, Steinbrenner also ordered him to ensure that postgame interviews were not conducted in the dampened locker room. But Cerrone was already envisioning how the Yankees would meet the press on the field.

"He says something along the lines of 'I don't want to hear from you that you've got to bring the media in here,'" Cerrone says. "What? C'mon. You know me, give me a little credit here, just have to make other arrangements."

A chaotic scene in the locker room during a World Series game was nothing new for Torre, who'd walked into his office in Game Two to find Steinbrenner and pitching coach Mel Stottlemyre sitting with Roger Clemens, who was crying after he'd thrown a bat at Piazza.

Four nights later, whether it was because the distractions of the Series were wearing him down, or simply the duel he was engaged in with Valentine, Torre had no interest in learning more about what had happened.

"Somebody came out and said that a pipe broke," Torre said afterward. "I didn't bother going back to check it because I really didn't care. I was concerned more of what was on the field."

At the time, some wondered if the actual story behind the busted pipes was juicier than officials let on.

The concept of pipes bursting at ancient Shea Stadium was believable enough—a pipe incident on Opening Day in 1999 flooded the Mets' locker room with raw sewage and resulted in $200,000 worth of repairs—but the *New York Post* surmised Steinbrenner might have had something to do with it in order to ensure a vacated locker room after the World Series game.

Everyone's suspicions were also heightened by the timing of the incident, which happened right after Neagle was pulled one out shy of qualifying for the win.

"It wasn't me, it wasn't me," Neagle told the *Post*, which reported multiple teammates suspected him of smashing the pipes.

In the end, it was just another surreal moment in a World Series filled with plenty of unforgettable weirdness. Asked in 2019 about the locker room flood and Steinbrenner's presence during the World Series, Torre grinned.

"Trust me," Torre says. "It wasn't boring."

***

Back on the dry diamond, both teams were glancing at the scoreboard and doing some math.

"There was urgency to that game, and every out you get into those games—even as a player, you do, you start counting outs," Yankees third baseman Scott Brosius says. "You start looking up, you're like, 'There's nine outs to go, how do we get those outs?'"

Valentine pulled his own starter, Bobby Jones, in favor of Glendon Rusch, who was the Mets' no. 4 starter in the regular season before thriving out of the bullpen in the playoffs. Rusch scattered three hits over two scoreless innings to lower his postseason ERA to 1.08. He ended the sixth by striking out Jose Canseco, the one-time 40-homer/40-steal man whose pinch-hitting appearance in place of Cone marked his only at-bat of the playoffs.

Torre replaced Cone with Nelson, who entered earlier than the seventh inning just three times in 73 regular-season appearances. But Torre was aggressive with his late-inning weapons throughout the 2000 playoffs. Nelson entered prior to the seventh inning four times in eight appearances, while Mike Stanton entered before the seventh inning twice in seven appearances, including in the fourth inning of Game Five of the AL Division Series, when Stanton earned the win with two scoreless innings.

"The Graeme Lloyds, the Mike Stantons, the Jeff Nelsons, they were all just tremendous during that run, really filling in the blanks when we really needed them," Cone says. "They were there. It was a lot. Those guys don't get enough credit."

Nelson gave up a leadoff single to Todd Zeile in the sixth, retired Robin Ventura on a flyout, and then snared a Benny Agbayani liner to begin an inning-ending double play. The out-counting grew more nerve-racking in the Mets dugout, where Valentine and his players knew the Yankees' Hall of Fame-bound closer, Mariano Rivera, loomed for the eighth.

In the seventh, Nelson struck out Jay Payton before Valentine began making his big moves. With right-handed-hitting Mike Bordick due up, Valentine called on lefty Lenny Harris to pinch-hit. Harris worked a six-pitch walk, after which Valentine utilized another pinch-hitter, left-handed-hitting Darryl Hamilton, for Rusch.

Once Hamilton was officially announced, Torre responded with his own move, pulling the right-handed Nelson for the left-handed Stanton. Valentine answered by pulling Hamilton and inserting Bubba Trammell, who struck out.

Valentine then set a World Series record by sending up his fourth pinch-hitter of the inning. But Kurt Abbott, batting in place of slumping rookie Timo Perez, struck out. The Mets were out of pre-Rivera outs to tie the score or take the lead.

"The idea of all the pinch-hitters and using the bench right there—I knew that we had to take every chance possible before Mariano," Valentine says. "Some people talk about that now, before the seventh inning, because pitchers are lined up for their last three. 'Oh boy, you've got to do something earlier.' Well, we were prepared to do that and it was fun."

Valentine made the rest of the moves available to him, utilizing his top two relievers, left-hander John Franco and closer Armando Benitez, in the eighth and ninth innings. Franco did his job by working around a leadoff single by Tino Martinez in a scoreless frame.

But, as the Mets feared he would, Rivera was going to do his job, too. Even though the pitcher's spot was due up second in the ninth, Torre didn't risk the eighth with Stanton or someone else. He called on Rivera for the ninth time in the 2000 playoffs and for the 37th time in the postseason since 1996. Torre would be asking Rivera to get more than three outs for the ninth time in October 2000 and for the 27th time since 1996.

"He's been pitching two innings to close out games a lot all year, so we pretty much knew he was going to come in," Jay Payton said afterward. "They were counting on us being shut down. They were counting on him not giving up a run, period."

Zeile singled with two outs in the eighth. Valentine used one of the two players left on his bench, Joe McEwing, to pinch-run for Zeile. McEwing and Zeile finished the 2000 regular season with the same number of stolen bases (three), but any little advantage was worth exploiting down one run and staring down a three-games-to-one deficit. Maybe McEwing, seven years younger, had a better chance of scoring from first on a double.

It didn't matter. Ventura popped out to end the eighth. Prior to the top of the ninth, Valentine made the last move he had at his disposal. The final player on the Mets' bench, Matt Franco, entered in the pitcher's spot while Benitez was double-switched into Zeile's no. 4 spot.

After Brosius worked a leadoff walk in the ninth, Rivera came up to bat for just the third time as a big leaguer. Appropriately, all three plate appearances came in a playoff game.

But instead of trying to lay down a bunt, or see a few pitches from the often-erratic Benitez, Rivera, who often playfully asked Torre if he could play center field, swung at the first pitch and flew out to right.

Derek Jeter followed with a liner to right that was misplayed into an error by Trammell, who was in the field after all of Valentine's machinations. Brosius and Jeter advanced a base on Luis Sojo's groundout before Benitez retired David Justice on a fly out.

A night that began with a leadoff homer by Jeter—the symbol of the relative ease with which everything seemed to come to the Yankees—was going to end with three players who symbolized the resourcefulness and resiliency of the Mets trying to scrape together a rally against the guy who made the hardest outs of the season look easy.

As Agbayani stepped to the plate, the word BELIEVE flashed on the scoreboard. But he struck out on four pitches and stared at his bat, as if he wanted to break it.

The popular underdog anthem, "Eye of the Tiger," blasted as Payton walked to the batter's box. Payton, just three nights removed from homering off Rivera, engaged the closer in a taut nine-pitch at-bat and fouled off back-to-back 3-2 pitches before Rivera won the battle by getting Payton to fly out to left.

Franco, who delivered a walk-off two-run single against Rivera to cap a raucous Mets win on July 10, 1999, was the Mets' last hope. But lightning did not strike twice. Rivera struck Franco out on four pitches, with Franco watching strike three sail by him at the knees.

Torre used five pitchers to throw 93 pitches over 6 ⅓ innings after Piazza's homer. He absorbed every move Valentine had at his disposal.

And in the end, Torre was right. A one-run lead was enough.

"God, that was a tough ballgame tonight," Torre said afterward.

The win was Torre's 45th in the playoffs with the Yankees. And it did not seem to be a coincidence, with the Yankees' dynasty appearing at its most imperiled, that it was the victory in which he relied most on his gut and his faith in the players who'd done so much to get those first 44 postseason wins.

"Joe was that kind of guy, that kind of a manager," David Cone says. "He managed the heartbeat more so than the numbers of the matchups. He played hunches. He would probably have a hard time in today's game, managing all the analytics nowadays. He would probably find a way—[he's] smart enough, he could probably do it. But he was definitely allowed, in that era, to manage by feel much more."

Even in defeat, Valentine had lived up to Zeile's assessment of his dugout demeanor by raising his game when opposed by the best in baseball. And despite losing to fall into a hole that only five teams had ever escaped in the World Series, the Mets admired, both in real time and with the benefit of hindsight, the managerial duel they'd just watched and their skipper's role in it.

"They both did a great job managing the game tonight," Payton said. "There was no advantage either way. They both made all the right moves and [did] everything that could possibly be done. And it just came down to the fact we weren't able to push another run across the plate."

"Without a doubt, you're seeing the two first-class managers in all of baseball, as far as I can see," Rusch said. "They're making the right moves and doing everything they need to do to help their teams win. They're just tight ballgames. That's all there is to it."

Added Lenny Harris in 2019: "Joe was trying to get the matchups, Bobby was trying to get the matchups. We had to use maybe two or three pitchers for one or two hitters, because they were so dominant on their side of the ball. Bobby had to play what he had, his hand. His hand wasn't trump-high or anything, but he made it work the best way he could."

And nearly two decades after their duel, what did the two differently wired rivals think about the night they turned a diamond into a chess-board?

"I did what I felt was right," Torre says.

"I thought it was amazingly fun," Valentine says.

# CHAPTER 5
# GAME FIVE

**Yankees 4, Mets 2**
**Yankees win series, four games to one**

**MIKE PIAZZA WASN'T** one to deliver a rah-rah speech to fire up his teammates, preferring instead to lead by example and let his play do the talking.

Or, on the afternoon before what turned out to be the final game of the 2000 season, let the music do the talking.

The guy who got Ozzy Osbourne's guitarist, Zakk Wylde, to perform the National Anthem before a 1999 game—and would wind down from his cathartic game-winning home run against the Braves on September 21, 2001, by spinning hard rock records with DJ Eddie Trunk at a New York City radio station—authorized the soundtrack for batting practice at Shea Stadium. Songs such as Aerosmith's "Livin' on the Edge," Creed's "Higher," and Journey's "Don't Stop Believin'" filled the air with thunder and bombast while serving as musical inspiration for the daunting task that lay ahead of the Mets.

By grinding out a 3–2 win in Game Four the night before, the Yankees became the 38th team to take a three-games-to-one lead in a best-of-seven World Series. Thirty-three of those teams won the World Series. Twenty of them won it in five games. Twelve needed a sixth or seventh game to do it.

In Mets math, of course, this meant only four of the 37 previous teams—a little less than 11 percent—won a best-of-seven World Series after falling behind three games to one. No one had done it since the 1985 Kansas City Royals, who stayed alive with a win in Game Five in St. Louis before going home and beating the Cardinals in two games.

If the Mets were going to make history, they'd have to win Game Five at Shea Stadium before going across town and winning two more games at Yankee Stadium, where the Yankees were 17–3 in playoff games since 1998 and 7–0 in World Series games since their most recent loss to the Atlanta Braves in 1996.

But miraculous comebacks were in the franchise DNA, and the core of the 2000 team had already mounted a stunning comeback to get into the playoffs the year before, when the Mets were two games out of the wild card spot with three games to play. Not even two weeks after that, the Mets fell behind the Braves three games to none in the NL Championship Series but won the next two games—"Don't Stop Believin'" blared and Shea Stadium shook just before Robin Ventura delivered his game-winning "Grand Slam Single"—and were twice three outs away in Game Six from becoming the first baseball team to climb out of that hole and force a seventh game.

Now the Mets just wanted to win one more game and get to Game Six and a rematch of Game Two, when NL Championship MVP Mike Hampton was outdueled by Roger Clemens before and after Clemens chucked a bat at Piazza. The Mets knew Hampton couldn't perform much worse than he'd done while giving up four runs and 13 baserunners over six innings. And who knew how the notoriously over-amped Clemens would perform if given two more days of pondering his next showdown with Piazza and his next chance to rewrite his post-season narrative?

"I think you draw on all your experiences, and we've had a lot of experiences, and we've had our backs against the wall," Bobby Valentine said following Game Four. "And tomorrow we're going to come out and give it our best shot. I just believe we can do that, and hopefully continue after that."

Across the field, the Yankees weren't comforted by the odds being overwhelmingly in their favor. Sure, almost 90 percent of the teams to go up three games to one in a best-of-seven World Series ended up raising the trophy.

But few teams reached Game Five with a chance to close out the World Series as narrowly as the Yankees, who earned each of their first three wins by a run apiece and outscored the Mets 15–14 in the first four games. It marked just the sixth time a team took a 3–1 World Series lead while possessing a run differential of plus-one or fewer and the fifth time all three wins were by one run.

The difficult path to a 3–1 World Series lead was appropriate for the Yankees, who navigated a far rockier road in 2000 than in their three previous championship seasons. The Yankees went just 23–28 from May 1 through June 30 before stumbling into the playoffs by losing 15 of their final 18 games.

"We had one of those spotted seasons, I guess," Joe Torre said before the game. "But when it came to postseason, we're where we wanted to be. I'm not sure about midseason, if we felt we'd be here."

The Yankees could lose Game Five and still retain home field advantage and head back to the Bronx as the favorites to close it out. But with their advantage over the Mets established as a razor-thin one, the Yankees knew a second loss at Shea Stadium could turn them into the team scrambling to regain its footing.

"When you go to the other ballpark, you get in a short series, in a seven-game series, momentum can change and sometimes you don't have enough time to turn it around," Paul O'Neill says. "You see the end line of winning, but it's hard to get there, winning four games. You don't get ahead of yourself."

Plus, these was the Mets they were facing. While the Yankees weren't the first team in franchise history to take a three-games-to-one lead in a Subway Series—the Yankees also did so against the Giants in 1936, when they won the Series in six games, and the Dodgers in 1941 and 1949, a pair of Series they won in five games—they were the first to do so against the Mets while being under the iron grip of George Steinbrenner. The Yankees were already facing win-or-else expectations from inside and outside the organization. A loss in Game Five would have added another layer of dread to a Series filled with trepidation.

One team up, 3–1, feeling as if it were in pure must-win mode in order to cement itself as a dynasty. One team down, 3–1, actually in pure must-win mode as it tried to extend its season and topple Goliath in the biggest and most resounding style possible.

The difference between ecstasy and misery was almost indistinguishable. It would take until the stroke of midnight, and a matchup between the two players who had traveled the farthest to become the symbol of their teams, to finally establish that line and bring the Subway Series to a memorable close.

***

Both managers tinkered with their lineups a night after Torre's lineup shuffle resulted in Derek Jeter's tone-setting leadoff homer. With Mets southpaw Al Leiter on the mound again, Torre sat Luis Sojo in favor of Game One star Jose Vizcaino, who batted leadoff while Jeter returned to the no. 2 spot.

Valentine's more extensive moves reflected the urgency of the Mets' situation against Yankees left-hander Andy Pettitte. Timo Perez, who was the Mets' best everyday player during the NLCS but was just 2-of-16 in the World Series, took a seat on the bench and was replaced atop the order by Benny Agbayani, who was hitting .326 in the playoffs while reaching base in all 13 games.

Perez was replaced in right field by Bubba Trammell, making his first start since September 24 and only his fifth start since September 1. And Mike Bordick, who started 55 of the Mets' final 61 regular-season games at shortstop following his acquisition from the Baltimore Orioles on July 28 but was just 4-for-33 in the playoffs, was benched in favor of utilityman Kurt Abbott.

The Yankees struck first for the fourth time in the series when Bernie Williams led off the second with a home run. But Valentine's moves paid off in the bottom of the inning. With one out, Trammell walked and Jay Payton singled. Abbott advanced the runners with a slow roller to shortstop, which initially seemed to all but extinguish the threat because it brought the notoriously light-hitting Leiter to the plate with two outs. Leiter was just 3-for-58 during the regular season and hitless in seven postseason at-bats.

But after watching ball one sail by, Leiter took a long glance down the third base line. On the next pitch, Leiter dropped down a surprise swinging bunt that landed in no-man's-land between the pitcher's mound and first base.

Pettitte raced immediately to cover the bag as Tino Martinez darted over to field the ball. Martinez then bobbled it as he looked up to Pettitte.

The throw, and Pettitte, still beat the slow-footed Leiter to the bag, but Pettitte also bobbled the ball as Leiter was called safe and Trammell scored the tying run. Pettitte was charged with the error.

The Mets needed just one more pitch, and one more Yankees miscue, to take the lead. Agbayani followed with a slow roller to third base, where Scott Brosius charged it and tried to make the Brooks Robinson-esque barehand play. But Brosius overran the ball as it skipped under him and into shallow left field while Payton scored the go-ahead run. Agbayani was credited with an infield single and an RBI.

As far as rallies go, it wasn't much. But it was an awfully Yankees way to build a rally, taking advantage of an opponent's mistakes and any little daylight they provided.

"Two slow rollers for the Mets here in the second and they've taken a one-run lead," Joe Buck said on the FOX telecast.

Added Tim McCarver: "Two rollers that traveled about 140 feet—70 feet each."

Staked to the lead he helped create, Leiter retired 10 of the next 12 batters he faced, a span in which he only allowed one runner to get as far as second base. The Mets generated a little more traffic against Pettitte, who allowed a leadoff single to Trammell in the fourth.

One out later, Pettitte battled Abbott for nine often-entertaining pitches before the new starting shortstop drew a walk. Abbott fouled off the fifth pitch of the at-bat, and his bat broke into two with the fat part skipping to shortstop as Pettitte crouched and put his hands in the air to protect himself. Jeter went into a fielding position as the bat neared him and nearly picked it up with his glove.

The FOX cameras captured Clemens spitting sunflower seeds and staring stoically ahead and Piazza grinning in the Mets' dugout. Jeter reached down and, with a small grin on his face, handed the bat to one of the Mets' bat boys.

But any chance the Mets had at creating momentum disappeared before Leiter could try and replicate his second-inning success. Pettitte, possessing the most lethal pickoff move in baseball, fired to first base, where Abbott was taking a far bigger lead—his back foot was near the curve in the grass along the infield dirt—than either Trammell or Payton had taken while Pettitte battled Payton in the second and Abbott one batter earlier. Abbott was out by plenty and Leiter followed with a groundout.

The Mets again stranded a pair of runners in the fifth, when Piazza doubled with two outs and Zeile was intentionally walked before Robin Ventura flew out.

The near misses raised the frustration and anxiety levels for both teams. O'Neill led off the fifth by battling Leiter over seven pitches, the last of which he hit in between second base and shortstop. Abbott, lacking the range of Bordick, needed an extra step or two to corral the ball and fire to first, where the baseball and O'Neill seemed to arrive at the same time.

But first base umpire Jerry Crawford called O'Neill out. O'Neill, his momentum taking him toward the right, gestured angrily before turning and beginning to argue with Crawford. First base coach Lee Mazzilli, trying to keep the right fielder in the game, twice pushed O'Neill away before Torre jogged out to first base to take up the case.

Had video review existed, O'Neill probably would have been sent back to first. Replays indicated O'Neill's foot hit the bag a split-second before the ball landed in Todd Zeile's glove. Instead, the Yankees remained more than halfway to defeat.

"The intensity is what I remember," O'Neill says. "You just go home not physically exhausted, just mentally exhausted, because you realize you really can concentrate on every single pitch when you get to that point of the year. You can't say that at the beginning of the year: 'Hey, I'm not going to give an at-bat away, I'm going to concentrate on every pitch over the course of a season.' That's physically impossible.

"Once you get to the playoffs, especially the World Series, it's reality. It happens. You're in every pitch and like I said, when you walk away at night, you're mentally exhausted."

Zeile, meanwhile, felt increasingly uneasy as the Mets missed numerous opportunities to extend their lead against Pettitte and the Yankees.

"I remember feeling like in the middle innings, middle-to-late innings, that we needed to get something going because I didn't like the feeling it was creating," Zeile says. "Can't let this go too long, they're going to find a way to get something across. The longer it goes, the more pressure that's on us and not them. They're playing with house money at that point. It's tough to win when you're in that situation and you start feeling it."

The Mets ran out of margin for error in the top of the sixth. With one out, Jeter—who else?—homered on a 2–0 pitch. The blast to left was a no-doubter, so much so that Leiter kicked the dirt as the ball left Jeter's bat, the Yankees began spilling out of their dugout to prepare to greet Jeter, and the normally emotionless shortstop did his version of a bat flip by tossing the bat to the side on his follow-through.

The Yankees didn't do any more immediate damage to Leiter, who worked around a two-out walk to Williams in the sixth and a leadoff walk to O'Neill leading off the seventh. The Mets continued to miss chances against Pettitte, who allowed back-to-back singles in the sixth but retired Agbayani on a grounder to strand two runners in scoring position. In the seventh, Alfonzo delivered a leadoff single before Pettitte set down the heart of the order—Piazza, Zeile, and Ventura—in a 19-pitch sequence that included a fly out and two strikeouts.

The whiff of Ventura ended the night for Pettitte, who threw 129 pitches and had just one 1-2-3 inning. But the Mets had only one hit in 12 plate appearances with runners on base following Agbayani's RBI single.

While the Mets couldn't score against Pettitte, chasing him still seemed to give them an advantage on a night in which both bullpens figured to be taxed following the Game Four chess match between Joe Torre and Bobby Valentine. Torre's first moves in Game Five didn't appear to be as seismic as pulling Denny Neagle for David Cone in Game Four.

Jose Vizcaino, whose regular-season mastery of Leiter earned him the starts in Games One and Five, was just 1-for-6 without getting the ball out of the infield against Leiter in the World Series before he was pinch-hit for by Chuck Knoblauch leading off the eighth. Mike Stanton entered in a double-switch in the bottom of the inning, with the left-hander batting first and Luis Sojo replacing Vizcaino in the field and batting ninth. Stanton threw a 1-2-3 eighth before the latter move proved to be the most prescient of the series—and maybe the entire dynasty—for Torre.

Leiter came within inches of never seeing Sojo. After striking out Tino Martinez and O'Neill to open the inning, Leiter got to a 2-2 count on Jorge Posada. The Yankees' catcher fouled off back-to-back pitches before taking a cutter that tailed just inside for ball three. After another foul, Posada took ball four, which landed in almost the same spot as ball three.

The ninth pitch of the at-bat was the 138th of the game for Leiter and brought to the plate Brosius, who saw just seven pitches in going hitless in his first three at-bats of the evening. John Franco began warming in the bullpen, but everyone at Shea Stadium understood Valentine was going to ride with Leiter.

"His stuff wasn't deteriorating and Al's strong as an ox," Valentine says. "He didn't need to get his rest for the next game and he wasn't going to blow out, and the matchup of him against Sojo was one that before the game I was preferring against anyone in that bullpen against Vizcaino."

"Leiter was such a horse and he was throwing real well that day," Brosius says. "His cutter was great. He was throwing it hard, he was getting it in there. He was tough. So it wasn't shocking at all that he was going to stay in the game."

Brosius knew he'd see cutters and hoped to pull something to the left side. On the third pitch of the at-bat, Brosius did his best Jeter imitation with an "inside out" swing that resulted in a line drive single to left field.

Piazza went to the mound to converse with Leiter, which gave Sojo time to trot down the first base line and get a . . . "pep talk" from Mazzilli, who implored him to swing at Leiter's first pitch.

"Lee Mazzilli would 'MF' me, like, 'MF, you gotta get it done,'" Sojo says, offering suitable shorthand for the world's most infamous 12-letter curse word. "He was telling me that you've got to take advantage of the first pitch, because I used to take the first pitch all the time. But OK, you MF me, I'm gonna get it done. I'm not gonna take this first pitch."

Of Sojo's recollections of the profane nature of his advice, Mazzilli said, "I don't remember *that.*" But he knew what he'd advised him.

"Be ready," Mazzilli says. "Be ready first pitch."

Sojo indeed swung at Leiter's cutter, his 142nd pitch of the night, and broke his bat while sending the offering back up the middle. Leiter, his delivery taking him closer to the first base side of the mound, reached back but could not get a glove on the ball and fell on the ground.

Abbott, at shortstop, and Alfonzo, at second base, converged in attempts to field the grounder. But the ball kept skipping, past the diving, range-challenged Abbott as well as a sliding Alfonzo, the latter of whom could not get to it in shallow center field.

"When he hit that ground ball, we all thought it was going to be just a routine ground ball," Jose Vizcaino says. "And it was just a seeing-eye groundball that, like he said, took two minutes to go through the infield and then no one catches it.

"It was crazy. You watch the replay again and you say, 'How'd that groundball pass by?'"

Posada raced around third as Payton charged the ball, picked it up, and threw, the momentum of which sent him flying toward the infield; Piazza moved a step or two toward third base in hopes of blocking the plate against his fellow catcher. The ball arrived as Posada began his slide, and Piazza might have had a shot at applying the tag in a bone-jarring collision were he positioned at the plate. Posada crouched as he started to slide, as if preparing his body for a crash into Piazza.

But the ball hit Posada on his left side and skittered into the Mets' dugout. That allowed Brosius, who was slowing down as he neared third base, to race home with an insurance run.

"The ball and the runner got there at the same time," Piazza said afterward. "It's just one of those things. Got to roll the dice and try to make the play."

Brosius, the Yankees' third baseman, raised his hands, clapped them together once, and pumped his right fist as he ran down the third base line. It was a scene reminiscent of Mets third baseman Ray Knight racing home alone down the third base line, his hands atop his head, with the winning run in Game Six of the 1986 World Series at Shea Stadium.

After crossing the plate, Brosius jumped and clapped his hands together four times before being engulfed by teammates.

"Luis gets a hit in such a huge, huge place in the game," Brosius says. "All of a sudden, the other team only has one last crack at it. And you know who you have to come in for that last crack. You feel pretty good."

An out by Sojo only would have gotten the game to the bottom of the ninth, but that might have been enough to get the Mets to a Game Six. If the game were tied, Jeff Nelson was going to enter instead of Mariano Rivera. Nelson warmed up several times before the ninth inning, and he, like Turk Wendell prior to his entrance in the 11th inning of Game One, already felt gassed before he'd even thrown a real pitch.

"Once I saw Sojo get the hit, I was like, 'Thank God,' because I think I went from throwing 95 to about 85 and I'm like, 'OK, this is probably going to Game Six because I don't have a whole lot coming out of this bullpen,'" Nelson says.

Sojo ended up at third base with another big broken-bat October hit that was as iconic as it was surreal. The Seattle Mariners were clinging to a 1–0 lead in the one-game AL West playoff against the California Angels on October 2, 1995, when Sojo stepped to the plate with two outs in the seventh inning. In an 0-2 hole against Mark Langston, Sojo hit a bases-clearing double just fair down the first base line before racing home himself for a "Little League grand slam" following an errant throw to the plate.

That hit all but locked up the Mariners' first playoff berth. This one put the Yankees three outs away from accomplishing something far larger.

"Seventy-five hops, but it worked," Sojo says.

Speaking about their possibly not-suitable-for-children discussion, Mazzilli grinned.

"I'm glad he listened to me," Mazzilli says.

Putting Sojo into position to record the biggest hit of the season was another example of the Casey Stengel-esque magic touch Torre possessed throughout the dynasty, and how he had a knack for doing just the right thing to outsmart an opponent who was otherwise his equal. Wrote Roger Kahn in *The Era*, which was published in 1993:

"[Dodgers manager Leo] Durocher was matchless across pennant races, keeping his players furious, focused, and sullen yet not mutinous. As Yankee manager, Stengel practiced necromancy. I don't believe you can say that about any baseball manager today."

On the other side, Leiter trudged off the mound with his glove tucked under his left arm as if it were a football. The 142 pitches were the most he'd thrown in a game since April 14, 1989, when, as a 23-year-old making his 20th career start with the Yankees, he was left in to throw 163 pitches on a rainy night by manager Dallas Green, who would precede Valentine as the Mets' skipper.

Whether it was coincidence or not, Leiter suffered a shoulder injury less than a month later. He battled various arm ailments over the next four-plus seasons and made just 15 more big-league starts through the end of the 1993 season.

Now, having reignited his career and pitching for his favorite childhood team just three days after his 35th birthday, Leiter had again pushed himself as far as possible, this time for a far better and more defensible reason. But he'd fallen short, and the enormity of the moment appeared to be hitting him on the bench. The usually active Leiter sat, his head hanging low and his body static except for what appeared to be his shoulders gently rising and falling.

"A horse, an absolute animal," Mike Bordick told *Newsday* after the game. "He made you proud to be a Met. He left nothing out there. When he came out, guys in the dugout had tears in their eyes. The way he pitched and the way he carried himself and convinced us before the game that we were going to win . . . I don't think I've ever seen a pitcher do anything like that."

Franco relieved Leiter and retired pinch-hitter Glenallen Hill to end the inning. The Mets entered the ninth inning faced with the task of scoring twice off Rivera, who'd blown just one of his 19 postseason save opportunities and had allowed more than one run in a playoff game just once—four nights earlier, when he came into a nonsave situation in Game Two.

But there was a flicker of hope for the Mets, who were scheduled to send up a pinch-hitter for Franco followed by the pesky Agbayani and their most complete and patient hitter, Alfonzo. And if anyone got on, Piazza would step to the plate as the potential tying or winning run.

Rivera needed just three pitches to strike out the pinch-hitter, Darryl Hamilton. But the normally precise closer then walked Agbayani on four pitches. Agbayani was the 233rd batter opposed by Rivera in the playoffs, just the 10th to draw a walk, and the first to do so during the 2000 postseason.

Alfonzo stepped to the plate to "Eye of the Tiger," just as Payton did with one out in the ninth inning the night before. Short of Piazza, there may not have been anyone else the Mets wanted to see at the plate against the best closer of all time.

Among Alfonzo's many skills was an innate ability to work the count as well as put the bat on the ball, especially with two strikes. Rivera wasn't going to fall into another deep count, but Alfonzo lofted a 1–2 pitch to right field, which allowed Agbayani—who had taken second on defensive indifference two pitches earlier—to tag up and get to third.

That set up a delicious and almost unprecedented clash of the titans—the Yankees' best vs. the Mets' best, the world's premier closer against the planet's hardest-hitting catcher—that hundreds of thousands of fans probably would have signed up for if they could have requested a single one-on-one battle to determine the World Series.

With the clock reading 11:59, Piazza strode to the batter's box in his familiar slow, almost languid style, tapping his shoes with his bat as he walked. Hours after he'd selected the hard rock pregame soundtrack, Piazza was accompanied to the plate by the sinister tones of Mötley Crüe's "Too Young To Fall In Love."

The first verse played as Rivera conferred with Jeter and Sojo near the pitcher's mound. Piazza, his stoic expression unchanged, fixed his wristbands as he lingered near the plate, never making eye contact with Posada.

With the conference over, Jeter and Sojo went back to their positions. Rivera stood atop the mound and Piazza took his place in the batter's box. Rivera reared back and fired a fastball down the middle. And as was his custom against almost everyone not named Greg Maddux, Piazza took the pitch, a called strike.

Piazza stepped briefly out of the batter's box. The clock struck midnight.

The Mets catcher stepped back into the batter's box, tapped home plate with his bat, and took a handful of mini swings. Rivera delivered his second pitch, a cutter. What happened next lasted only six seconds, but no one in the park is likely to forget where they were for those six seconds, or what they were thinking. It was the baseball version of an inkblot test, one taken by tens of thousands of people seeing something different in the same thing.

Piazza swung and crushed the ball to center field. The FOX cameras perched behind home plate arched high, tracking the ball as it flew high into the air.

"Piazza gets into one . . .," FOX play-by-play man Joe Buck said.

In right field, Paul O'Neill began preparing for extra innings.

"One hundred percent—off the bat I thought it was gone," O'Neill says.

At third base, Brosius also feared the worst.

"I thought he hit it, I did," Brosius says. "I remember kind of almost catching Jeter's eye, like, 'Uh-oh.'"

"He hit that ball and I screamed—I'm surprised nobody got it on camera—[and] I said 'NO!!!'" Torre says. "Because I was sure it was out of the ballpark. He hit a ball in the air, it never came down. It never came down."

But almost as soon as it went up, it began coming down. Center fielder Bernie Williams trotted back casually.

"I was lean[ing] in the dugout like this," David Justice says, mimicking the body language he used to try to will the ball to stay in the park. "Because as soon as Piazza hit it, I thought it was gone.

"Then I just knew, as soon as I saw what Bernie was doing, I said, 'Oh, that's it. That's it.'"

So, too, did Zeile, standing on deck for an at-bat he was realizing he'd never get to take.

"I always had good success against Mo; I wanted to have a chance to face him," says Zeile, who at that point in his career was 5-for-16 with only two strikeouts against Rivera. "The ball left Mike's bat [and] I thought—I knew that it was playing deep and heavy air, and Shea in center field at that time of the night and that time of the year, you've got to hit a rocket. It's not like the other balls during the season.

"And so when it went in the air, I kind of hoped more than I thought that it was going to get over Bernie's head. And then when I saw him slow down, I'm like, 'This one's over.'"

Williams continued gliding back but slowed his pace as he put up his glove.

". . . into center, back is Bernie Williams . . .," Buck said.

Williams caught the ball. The clock had officially struck midnight on the Mets. For only the third time in history, the World Series ended with a Hall of Fame-bound pitcher retiring a Hall of Fame-bound hitter for the final out.

As for the Yankees' standing in history? There was no longer any doubt.

"A three-peat," Buck said.

The Yankees were a dynasty—the first team in baseball to win three consecutive titles since the Oakland Athletics of 1972–74 and the first to win at least four championships in five seasons since the Yankees won five straight under Casey Stengel from 1949 through 1953.

And to ensure their spot in baseball annals, the Yankees had stared down the worst-case scenario of their fans and their owner.

"World Series titles mean more to everybody, but [in] that particular case, yeah, I think it would have been that much sweeter for the Mets," says David Cone, who pitched for the Mets from 1987 until 1992. "For the Yankees, it was more relief. I think we enjoyed it, but I think it was more relief that we got through it, we kept it going. It wasn't like '96—the first one, it's exhilarating. '98, all-time great team. '99, back-to-back. And 2000 was relief, we got through it.

"And it was the Mets."

Rivera raised his arms in the air and jumped three times before exchanging an awkward hug with Tino Martinez, who leaped for Rivera as the closer landed. Jeter, who would be named the World Series MVP after hitting .409 with a pair of homers, leaned back, à la Justice in the dugout, as the ball flew toward center field. He began jumping backward as Williams settled underneath the ball. Once it was caught, Jeter turned, jumped, and leaped into a hug with Sojo.

The rest of their teammates poured out of the dugout and the bullpen. A team that carried itself with a weariness and a self-inflicted burden of championship-or-bust expectations could finally express pure, unfiltered joy.

"It's hard to express, as a player, the elation," Brosius says. "It doesn't matter who you're facing—[whether it's] the Braves, it's the Padres, it's the Mets, all those guys. Doesn't matter who you're facing. The elation of winning, for me, anyway, was like the number-one feeling that you feel, like all the hard work was worth it."

Much like Cleon Jones 31 years and a few hundred feet to his left earlier, Williams went to one knee in center field. To his right, O'Neill, now a five-time World Series champion, did the same—an acknowledgment that a yearly goal, one that was infused with a more personal meaning in 2000, had been achieved.

O'Neill's Dad, Charles, died of a long illness the morning of October 27, 1999—the same night the Yankees were going to try and complete a four-game World Series sweep of the Atlanta Braves. His wife, Nevalee, called Torre and told him her husband had to play as the Yankees tried to complete a sweep. As the Yankees celebrated following their 4–1 win, O'Neill wept into Torre's arms before heading home with his family.

One day shy of one year later, it took O'Neill less than a minute to don a World Series hat before he wrapped Tino Martinez in a bear hug.

"Once Bernie caught it, I was just like, 'Yeah,' because I remember I lost my father in '99 and I didn't get to really enjoy that World Series," O'Neill says. "I was just hoping that I got to another one. At that point, I just remember I got to another one and I really got to enjoy it."

All the tears were of the happy variety this time. Most were shed by Torre, who began to cry by the time the Yankees hoisted him upon their shoulders and carried him off the field. The New York kid who returned home to win his first World Series put the bow on top of his Hall of Fame résumé by returning to the site of his first managerial stop to win his fourth title.

"It was unbelievable, a New York kid winning, first off, with the Yankees," Torre says. "But at Shea Stadium, where I started my managing career—it was much different in that visiting dugout, I can tell you that."

He had that right.

Even as the flight of his ball slowed, Piazza continued running toward first base. Williams made the catch as Piazza neared the bag. The catcher stopped just short of the base, turned, and walked into the dugout, never once glancing back at the celebration unfolding behind him.

The ability to witness the celebration was left to those who lingered in the dugout. Mike Hampton, the impending free agent who would never throw another pitch for the Mets, stood with his arms crossed. Lenny Harris and Matt Franco stood a few feet away while Joe McEwing sat on the bench behind them.

"I was so stunned about it, because I was like, what else can happen next?" Harris says. "For the whole series, we're leading, we just didn't put the pedal on the medal and blow the games out. We just kept them around."

Valentine walked up and down the dugout, occasionally looking toward the field. Alfonzo watched from a seat on the bench.

"It was a very weird feeling to have it end, when, up to that very second, I think we all felt like we still had some oxygen in our lungs and a breath to take," Zeile says. "It really sucks, seeing people celebrate on your home field.

"I still tried to experience the whole experience of it. I sat and watched them celebrate. I tried to, instead of just being miserable about us not winning, I tried to imagine what it would feel like to be in that moment."

Within minutes, the Mets were in their locker room, trying to put the game, the series, the season, and an era into context.

"It was an honor to catch that ball game, because he really pitched lights-out," Piazza said of Leiter. "It's very frustrating when it comes up short. But that's the heart that Al has and that's the heart this club has."

As for his last at-bat of the season?

"I hit it well," Piazza said. "You can only hit it. You can't guide it. It was one of my better swings off him. And just whatever it did, it stayed up. Just didn't have enough to get it in the gap or over his head.

"So what can you do? I hit it well. That's all you can say."

Piazza remained at his locker for almost 20 minutes. At least seven times, he uttered, "What can you say?"—a four-word phrase that expressed nothing and everything.

"I think losing, period . . .," Piazza said before pausing. "It's just painful."

Valentine remained dressed in his full uniform 90 minutes after the game. He stood at the entrance to the locker room, shaking hands with everyone—players, officials, reporters—as they exited.

But for Valentine's players, the task of coming to grips with the end of their season was just beginning.

"I think I didn't get over it for about three weeks," McEwing says. "I sat in my locker for two-and-a-half hours after the game, just drained mentally and physically. And I was a bench guy. Mentally and physically just drained."

Piazza's backup, Todd Pratt, offered a glimpse into the post-defeat rationalization process.

"I'm very disappointed in losing, especially being my second World Series and coming up short twice," said Pratt, who was with the Philadelphia Phillies when they fell to the Toronto Blue Jays in the 1993 World Series. "But the good thing about it is I get to go home and not watch any more baseball. We lost, but we lost to the best team."

Inevitably, there were questions about what the Mets thought of the Yankees' feat. Robin Ventura, always laconic, offered a direct response.

"Yeah, if you considered the Bulls [a dynasty], they're one," Ventura said, referring to the Michael Jordan-led NBA team that twice won three straight titles in the 1990s.

But . . .

"I don't know right now," Ventura said. "I don't care."

Qualifying what Ventura and his teammates had accomplished was a far more complicated endeavor. American sports fans are conditioned to believe there is only one winner—the champion. Valentine indicated as much in the hours before Game Five, when a reporter asked if New York should consider throwing a parade for both the Yankees and Mets regardless of who won the World Series.

"Actually, I told my guys the other day that there's a parade and that we are going to be the only team in it," Valentine said.

But Torre, despite his experience atop parade floats and the years he'd spent working under win-or-bust owner George Steinbrenner, was far more open to the idea of celebrating both teams.

"I've always had this problem when the Buffalo Bills couldn't win the Super Bowl," Torre said of the NFL team that made a record four straight Super Bowls from 1991 through 1994 but lost all of them. "But goddamn, they got there like four or five times, whatever it was.

That's a hell of an accomplishment. I think getting to the World Series should be celebrated. Unfortunately, somebody is going to win and somebody's going to lose. The team that loses gets that tag of being a loser.

"But I don't look at it that way. I think both clubs should be very proud of what we've accomplished getting here, because it's not easy getting here."

A five-game World Series usually goes down as a relatively easy victory for the champions. But the Mets made the Yankees' triumph a particularly hard-earned one. Each of the Yankees' wins were by two runs or fewer. They were only the second team, after the 1915 Boston Red Sox, to clinch a World Series in five or fewer games and record all four wins by two runs or fewer.

Coming close and making the Yankees grind out the hardest of their four championships was not much consolation for the Mets. But it would have to do, even if the battle for ultimate bragging rights was lost.

"It was a five-game series that felt like it was seven and felt like it was a 15-round boxing match," Zeile says. "At the end of the day, it's a five-game series and not a seven-game series."

Speaking after the game, Pratt held his thumb and pointer finger millimeters apart.

"Me and Matt Franco were saying they pitched that much better, they hit that much better, and they ran the bases this much better," Pratt said. "You can't say they overwhelmed us.

"Years from now, they'll say it was a 4–1 series. But . . ."

Pratt paused.

"They knew we were out there."

They did, then and now.

"This, by far, was the best team we played in the five years I've been here," Jeter said following Game Five. "All five games could have gone either way. We were just able to come up with a few more runs."

"I know we beat them in five games, but they were good," Torre said in 2019. "They were good. There was a lot to fear there."

The Mets were left to wonder whether outsiders would appreciate just how far they'd traveled and how much they'd accomplished. The same would be pondered by any World Series runner-up.

"How many things have to go right, from February 1 to November 1, basically?" says McEwing, who is now a coach with the Chicago White Sox. "How many things have to go right, injury-wise, player-wise, career years, down years, the help from people in the minor leagues, the help of trades?

"It's the importance of everybody, from top to bottom, being on the same page. And I think that's extremely important, because we're not just going to need the guys in this clubhouse right now. We're going to need the guys in the minor leagues, we're going to need the guys on the outside so that scouts [are] looking at other teams and seeing how that fits to your club. I use it all the time. All the time. So many things have to go right."

There were no parades for the Mets and no boisterous banner-raising ceremony prior to the 2001 home opener. Rusty Staub, who played for the Mets from 1973 to 1975 and again from 1981 to 1985, raised the National League pennant with assistance from Ralph Kiner, a beloved broadcaster for the team who spent his entire playing career with the Pittsburgh Pirates, and the mascot, Mr. Met.

"We haven't gotten enough credit for what we did," Valentine said following the 2001 home opener. "But we're in New York City and we didn't win the World Series. I understand."

But Valentine has sensed a growing appreciation for those Mets over the subsequent two decades. Unfortunately for the Mets, the 2000 run has grown in stature because the Mets have endured 11 losing seasons while qualifying for the playoffs three times and reaching the World Series just once over the course of 19 seasons since then.

And the club's modest beginnings are baked into the upbringing of all Mets fans, many of whom recognize the value of the journey even when the destination is not reached.

"Many people younger than me—but not young, because otherwise they wouldn't have been around—but most young ones and some who are older tell me that they appreciated those teams as much as any teams they've ever watched in baseball," Valentine says. "There is something really cool about those teams. There was something very, very different and cool."

Indeed, those Mets took perhaps the longest and most eventful path to a World Series defeat. They were only the seventh team in the division play era to reach the World Series the year after losing in the League Championship Series. Five of their predecessors won the championship, and the two who didn't—the 1980–81 Yankees and the 1997–98 Atlanta Braves—still had core players who were three years removed from winning a championship.

In addition, the 1999 Mets had mounted two stunning comebacks—first from a two-game deficit in the wild card race with three games to play and then from a three-games-to-none hole in the NLCS to get to extra innings of Game Six—which brought them to the brink of the World Series before taking the next step in 2000.

"I loved that team, I loved the '99 team," Valentine says. "I wanted those guys to be in the biggest stage, think that they belonged and go away with their heads up and their chest out. And I think that's what I might have said to them when we didn't win."

Winning it all once—never mind three times in a row or four times in five years—means a team doesn't have to worry about being appreciated by those that write the history of their era. But the Yankees establishing themselves as a dynasty also provided an opportunity, in real time and over the subsequent years, to examine why they had succeeded where no one else had done so in a generation.

For the Yankees, the 1998, 1999, and 2000 championship runs were fueled by the sting of losing to the Cleveland Indians in a five-game 1997 AL Division Series—a series the Yankees led two games to one and were four outs away from winning in Game Four before Mariano Rivera gave up the first of his two postseason homers, a game-tying blast to Sandy Alomar.

The series ended with a 4–3 loss in Game Five in which O'Neill doubled with two outs in the ninth before Williams flied out—to the track, this time in left field.

"When we lost to Cleveland in Game Five, there was so much devastation," Torre says. "I had to peel Bernie off the steps. He made the last out. You can't teach that."

"I don't think '98, '99, 2000 happen without the disappointment of '97," O'Neill says. "That's just probably as disappointed as I've ever been on a baseball field, because you win in '96, you get back to the playoffs, you assume that it's just going to happen again. And then you lose in Cleveland the way we did and it's just like you're in shock, you're just numb. Now you have to go back to spring training [and] go through a whole season just to get back to that point again."

Brosius, who was acquired from the Oakland Athletics following the season in exchange for free agent bust Kenny Rogers in what appeared to be a swap of players in need of fresh starts, noticed the determination during his first spring training.

"'We're getting back to the World Series, we're getting back to the World Series'—that was all they were concerned about," Brosius says. "It wasn't about personal goals. It wasn't about this or it wasn't about that. 'We're getting back to the World Series.' That was so refreshing. I just remember coming home and talking to my wife and just going, 'This is so cool over here. It's just about winning.'"

But while it was all about winning, the Yankees took a more treacherous postseason path than any previous dynasty. While the Casey Stengel-directed seven-time champions played in an era in which the playoffs consisted solely of the World Series and the 1972–74 Athletics had to win both the AL Championship Series and the World Series, the Yankees had to navigate three rounds of playoffs in order to emerge victorious.

The Yankees played 61 playoff games between 1996 and 2000, two fewer than Stengel's Yankees played from 1949 through 1960. The four members of the dynasty teams—Bernie Williams, Mariano Rivera, Andy Pettitte, and Paul O'Neill—who were also on the Yankees when they lost in the 1995 AL Division Series and the 2001 World Series were part of an additional 22 playoff games.

How did the Yankees not only get to the playoffs in all those seasons, but then thrive in the additional games played at the highest intensity and with the smallest margins for error?

Rivera provided a poignant glimpse into the mind-set he and his teammates shared in July 2019, when, during a conference call prior to his induction into the National Baseball Hall of Fame, he was asked about dealing with the grind of a season and succeeding in the playoffs.

"When you want to do something different, when you want to be there for your teammates, when you want to want as many championships as you can, you will do whatever it takes to continue pushing forward. Yes, we get tired. Physically, we get tired. But mentally, we were strong. Our heart was strong. So we didn't allow fatigue or a game perhaps that we lost to intervene in our process. We have a goal, we have a mentality that was different than many others. Our mentality was winning and then to have that type of mentality, you will find a way to get it done."

O'Neill nodded as he read Rivera's quote.

"It was the mentality of those teams," O'Neill says. "We were put together to win. And not every team has that culture, where winning, if you don't win the World Series, you were a failure. A lot of teams feel like if they had a good year, we had a good year. A good year's winning the World Series. And that was the difference."

Presented Rivera's quote, Torre appeared to well up.

"Strong—that's strong," Torre says. "They were unbelievable.

"I told them more than a few times in spring training, because the expectations were so high, it wasn't about ability. It was about character. And nobody would allow anything to get in the way."

The focus remained crystallized even as key players and figures dealt with difficult off-field issues during the playoff runs. In 1996, Torre's brother, Frank, received a heart transplant the day before the Yankees' World Series-clinching Game Six win over the Braves. In 1998, Darryl Strawberry was diagnosed with colon cancer during the AL Division Series against the Texas Rangers. Over the final six weeks of the 1999 season, Brosius, O'Neill, and Luis Sojo all lost their fathers. General Manager Brian Cashman missed the 2000 World Series clincher because his mother-in-law had just died.

"Paul and I and Luis, we shared a common thread, obviously, with what was going on," Brosius says. "Losing a dad in the middle of a season is not easy. It's a tough thing. But we were teammates. But we were friends. And we'd been through the wars together and so I think there's an element that we knew we had each other's back.

"And then I think there's an element that the field becomes your sanctuary."

The dynastic Yankees were also about the ability of management—from Gene Michael, who served as general manager during George Steinbrenner's suspension, to his successors, Bob Watson and Cashman—to not only acquire core members with those traits, but also fill in around them with players who understood what they were entering.

While long-time role players such as Sojo, Vizcaino, and Glenallen Hill fit easily into their reserve spots with the Yankees, high-profile players with difficult reputations such as Roger Clemens, Chuck Knoblauch, Darryl Strawberry, Wade Boggs, and Jose Canseco all contributed to one or more titles. Of those five players, only Clemens maintained the type of stature with the Yankees that he enjoyed elsewhere.

Whether it was skilled advance scouting or simply fate, the Yankees also missed out on acquiring Sammy Sosa and Juan Gonzalez, both of whom possessed immense power but had also alienated teammates at previous stops, in June 2000 before acquiring the less-accomplished but lower-maintenance David Justice. He went on to hit 20 homers in just 78 regular-season games before winning AL Championship Series MVP honors.

"It was funny—seems like that every part they added during that whole time fit perfectly," O'Neill says. "And it was because the personalities that we brought in fit in for what was going on here. It wasn't like anybody was coming in and was going to change what was going on here, because they were bigger than that. No. Everybody kind of humbly walked in to be a part of this team. We had enough names and enough people that people just immediately realized their job was to play and play well enough that we win."

And the Yankees did that more, and better, than anyone else in the last 40 years.

"Winning four World Series out of five years, in this day and age when you have to come through layer after layer of postseason play, we can put our record, our dedication, our resolve up against any team that's ever played the game of baseball in my mind," Torre said following the Game Five win. "We may not have the best players. But we certainly have had the best team."

# CHAPTER 6

# THE SUBWAY SERIES SINCE THE SUBWAY SERIES

**NEW YORKERS WAITED** 44 years for a Subway Series, so in true Big Apple fashion, fans began anticipating a rematch around the moment Mike Piazza's fly ball landed in Bernie Williams's glove for the final out of the 2000 season.

The Yankees, of course, were the champions, having proven, even in a wounded, diminished state, that they deserved to be the favorites until somebody actually knocked them off. Their entire everyday lineup was coming back, as were the top three members of the rotation—Roger Clemens, Orlando Hernandez, and Andy Pettitte—plus, of course, the great closer Mariano Rivera.

And why couldn't the Mets once again be the team that tried to topple the dynasty? The Mets had a couple more question marks than the

Yankees—three-fifths of the rotation was scheduled to hit free agency, and they had to find a new shortstop and right fielder.

But the most eagerly anticipated free agency of all time was about to commence, and Alex Rodriguez, hitting the open market at age 25, openly publicized the fact that he'd grown up a Mets fan (even though he was raised in Florida) and rooted for Keith Hernandez (even though Rodriguez played shortstop and Hernandez was a Gold Glove-winning first baseman). One way to cover up for a rotation lacking a true ace would be to sign Rodriguez to play shortstop and pair him with Piazza in the middle of the lineup.

Yet barely two weeks after the World Series, the dream of Rodriguez suiting up for the Mets evaporated. After meeting with Rodriguez's agent, Scott Boras, at the general manager meetings in mid-November, Steve Phillips held a conference call to declare the Mets were no longer pursuing the superstar shortstop.

Phillips said Boras made it clear that in addition to the record-shattering contract it would take to land Rodriguez, the Mets would also have to provide Rodriguez his own office at Shea Stadium as well as his own marketing staff. Phillips also indicated he was told that Rodriguez wanted use of a private jet and what he described as a "billboard presence in the city."

The demands of Boras and/or Rodriguez likely would have stunned any general manager, but especially one whose best player was a decidedly no frills superstar. The one perk Piazza was afforded was use of the small extra room behind his locker at Shea Stadium, where Piazza stored some of his extra equipment and listened to hard rock records without being needled by his teammates for his passé musical tastes. Occasionally, Piazza would ask if he could bring his dad and youngest brother into the locker room.

To bring in Rodriguez and acquiesce to his demands would, in Phillips's mind, immediately put Rodriguez on an island inside the Mets' clubhouse.

"I have serious reservations that a structure in which you have a

24-plus-one-man roster can really work," Phillips said. "In fact, I don't think it can work."

Without Rodriguez—who ended up signing with the Texas Rangers for 10 years and $252 million, the latter of which was twice as lucrative as the previous richest contract in sports history—the Mets mostly stood pat. While the Mets re-signed no. 3 starter Rick Reed, utilityman Lenny Harris, and popular relievers John Franco and Turk Wendell, they watched ace Mike Hampton depart for the Colorado Rockies and fifth starter Bobby Jones sign with the San Diego Padres. Hampton and Jones were replaced by a pair of free agents, Kevin Appier and Steve Trachsel.

But making small moves to supplement their core didn't work for the Mets, who rendered talk of a Subway Series rematch irrelevant for most of the season. Robin Ventura collected 62 RBIs, his fewest since his rookie season in 1990. Todd Zeile hit 10 homers, his fewest since 1992. Rey Ordonez, who missed the final three-plus months of the 2000 season with a broken arm, was not exactly Rodriguez with the bat. The 20-something-year-old outfielders—Benny Agbayani, Jay Payton, and Timo Perez—did not build off their late-season success in 2000.

The Mets fell under .500 with a 10–0 loss to the Montreal Expos five games into the season and were 10 games under by May 17. They spent most of the summer fending off the Expos for fourth place in the NL East and began rebuilding at the trade deadline, when core players Reed, Wendell, Dennis Cook, and Todd Pratt were traded.

"We didn't have the same passion level," Phillips says. "Even though we didn't win a World Series, there was a sense that we sort of proved something, that we were better than just a good little team. We stood toe-to-toe with the best. And I think as I look back, I don't know that we had the same edge in 2001. We just couldn't get it going."

The Yankees' machine, meanwhile, continued humming. Their veteran everyday players produced as expected except for Chuck Knoblauch, who hit .250 after his throwing yips forced a move to left field.

Knoblauch was replaced at second base by rookie Alfonso Soriano, who hit 18 homers and stole 43 bases.

The big off-season addition for the Yankees was Mike Mussina, who signed a six-year deal worth $88.5 million as a free agent. The former Orioles ace went 17–11 with a 3.15 ERA, a performance valued at a team-high 7.1 wins above replacement by Baseball-Reference.com (Appier and Trachsel combined for a 4.4 WAR). Mussina also came within a strike of throwing a perfect game against the Boston Red Sox September 2 before ex-Mets outfielder Carl Everett delivered a pinch-hit single.

But Mussina wasn't the AL Cy Young Award winner in 2001. Roger Clemens received that honor. Clearly more comfortable in his surroundings after being a part of two World Series winners and shedding his shaky postseason reputation the previous fall, Clemens won 16 straight decisions on his way to going 20–3—his sixth 20-win season—with a 3.51 ERA and taking home his record sixth Cy Young.

None of his 33 starts, though, were at Shea Stadium. Clemens was in line to face the Mets on the road in mid-June, but Joe Torre shuffled the rotation so that Clemens wouldn't get what was lining up to be a Sunday Night Baseball start against Piazza and the Mets.

Torre sarcastically told reporters he was sorry to cost ESPN the chance to tout the baseball version of "Muhammad Ali-Joe Frazier," this match that cannot be missed.

"I saw an example in the World Series of what can be built up, and it was a little frightening to me," Torre said. "I don't see any need to have that happen again."

The Yankees spent most of the first half hovering in second place in the AL East before moving past the Boston Red Sox for good on July 3, the day before George Steinbrenner's birthday. On September 8, the Yankees opened up a season-high 12-game lead on the Red Sox while the suddenly surging Mets won for the 17th time in 21 games to land within a game of .500 at 71–72 and remained seven games out of first place in the middling NL East.

But any thoughts of an unlikely Subway Series rematch were about to be overshadowed in the most tragic fashion possible.

On the morning of September 11, Torre woke up and prepared to attend a charity luncheon prior to the opener of the Yankees' three-game series against the Chicago White Sox. But his driver arrived, told Torre the event was sure to be cancelled, and recommended he put on his television. A little under 400 miles to the west, where the Mets were getting ready to play the Pittsburgh Pirates, Mets players and staff members awoke to phone calls telling them to do the same thing.

America was under attack. Nineteen members of al-Qaeda hijacked four airplanes—two taking off from Boston's Logan Airport and one apiece from the airports in Newark, New Jersey, and Dulles Airport in suburban Washington, DC. Two of the planes were flown into the World Trade Center's Twin Towers 17 minutes apart—at 8:46 and 9:03 a.m. Both towers would collapse within 90 minutes of impact.

Another hijacked plane was crashed into the Pentagon at 9:37 a.m. Twenty-six minutes later, the fourth plane, believed to be headed for the White House or the Capitol, crashed into a field in Shanksville, Pennsylvania, less than 90 miles southeast of Pittsburgh. It is believed passengers on the fourth plane, aware of the three earlier crashes, tried overtaking the hijackers, who drove the plane into the ground.

The worst terrorist attacks in American history killed 2,977 people and injured more than 25,000. Hundreds more would battle and succumb to 9/11-related cancers and illnesses. The War on Terror was launched October 7, 2001, and continues nearly two decades later.

Baseball commissioner Bud Selig quickly postponed Tuesday's schedule and wasted little time subsequently postponing the rest of the week's games. The NFL eventually followed suit with its games scheduled for September 16–17, but only after New York's teams, the Jets and Giants, threatened to boycott and forfeit if they were forced to play.

With flights cancelled nationwide, the Mets booked a bus to get home from Pittsburgh. As the silent bus reached New York City, players saw the empty skyline and smelled the awful stench of Ground Zero.

Upon reaching Shea Stadium, the Mets saw their home had been turned into a staging area, where Bobby Valentine was coordinating around-the-clock efforts to collect rescue supplies.

Players from both New York teams took trips to local hospitals, the National Guard Armory, other staging areas, and, eventually, Ground Zero itself, uncertain what they could do but hoping to help in any way possible, even if it was to simply provide a hug or a few minutes of baseball conversation.

"The Armory was probably the most powerful [moment], because that's where all the loved ones were waiting for word, the DNA results just to verify their loved ones are gone," Torre said in 2019. "That was tough."

Valentine hoped for the first few days that the rescue efforts would yield survivors. But as the hours ticked by, reality began setting in.

"Those four days that seemed like four months, they were the most depressing days of my life," Valentine says. "It was a rescue effort. And we rescued no one. It was so disappointing. I remember when the team left on their charter, I was going to fly commercially to Pittsburgh, to make a point that you could fly commercial again and all that stuff.

"But I was really hoping that before I got on the plane, someone's going to be rescued, because they were saying this is the time. If they don't get them now, they're going to be gone. I was counting the minutes before I got into the plane hoping that."

Even as players wondered if it was too soon to return to the field, baseball resumed September 17 with the Mets in Pittsburgh and the Yankees' series against the White Sox shifted to Chicago. Four days later, baseball returned to New York, where the Mets and Atlanta Braves would play the first post-9/11 sporting event in the Big Apple.

The fierce rivals were now bonded by something unimaginable: trepidation at playing the game they loved. A baseball stadium, forever a place of respite and escape, was now viewed as a terrorist target—especially Shea Stadium, where the soundtrack of a baseball game inevitably included the roar of airplanes flying above as they departed from or arrived at nearby LaGuardia Airport.

"I think everybody who was wearing an Atlanta Braves uniform was scared to death," Braves star Chipper Jones told *Sports Illustrated* in 2016. "We wanted to be with our families, but we would not allow our families to come to New York. What better way to have a secondary attack or wave, where you could take out as many people as possible, than at a professional baseball game where you had 40 to 50,000 people in the stands. It just seemed like the prime target considering also the proximity to LaGuardia Airport."

Just 11 months earlier, two fans had managed to get onto the field and join in the Yankees' celebratory pile near the pitcher's mound at Shea Stadium. Such a lighthearted act of law breaking was now impossible to comprehend. Ten nights after the worst day in American history, fans would be walking through metal detectors inside a building ringed by heavy security and watched overhead by snipers positioned atop the roof.

"Playing that game at Shea Stadium was scary," Valentine says. "And no one in their right mind wanted to play that game. And luckily, it took two teams who are crazy enough to play and make [it] happen."

Both teams lined up along their respective baselines for ceremonies that included Marc Anthony's rendition of the National Anthem and Diana Ross performing "God Bless America." A 21-gun salute took place in a silent stadium, and the NYPD's bagpipe troupe performed "God Bless America" and "The Caissons Go Rolling Along." Cameras captured Mets superstar Mike Piazza weeping. Jones would admit he glanced downward so that nobody could see the tears welling in his eyes.

After the ceremonies concluded, the Mets—sporting first responder hats over the objections of Major League Baseball—and Braves crossed the field and exchanged handshakes and hugs. In the seventh inning,

Liza Minnelli performed "New York, New York" as a group of police officers and firefighters danced to the beat, like a kick line, behind her. Following her performance, Minnelli hugged the Mets' on-deck batter, Jay Payton.

An inning later, the Braves took a 2–1 lead when regular Mets foil Brian Jordan laced a tie-breaking RBI double off Armando Benitez. In the bottom of the eighth, with Queens native Steve Karsay pitching for the Braves, Edgardo Alfonzo drew a walk with one out to bring up Piazza.

As he usually did, Piazza took the first pitch, a 94-mph strike on the outside corner. Karsay's next offering was another fastball near the same location, but Piazza reached out, swung, and launched the most iconic homer of his career, if not the most iconic homer in New York history.

"This one has a chance!" yelled Mets television play-by-play man Howie Rose as the ball continued soaring in the air, not landing until it bounced off the camera stands well beyond the center-field fence.

Shea Stadium shook with fans who were smiling, laughing, and shedding tears of joy—emotions that seemed out of reach just hours earlier. Fifteen years later, the enormity of Piazza's homer would be underlined by its inclusion on his Hall of Fame plaque, which ended with these words: "Led Mets to the 2000 Subway Series, and helped heal a nation one year later with his dramatic home run in the first Mets game in New York following the 9/11 terror attacks."

Said Piazza during his induction speech: "Many of you give me praise for the two-run home run on the first game back on September 21st to push us ahead of the rival Braves. But true praise belongs to police, firefighters, first responders, who knew they were going to die, but went forward anyway."

In the cathartic aftermath of Piazza's homer, his manager thought back to the last pitch of the previous year's World Series.

"I could tell you every home run off the bat, I knew was a home run," Valentine says. "And that [in 2000] was a home run. And I can't explain it."

A laughing Valentine then began to explain it.

"Somebody was trying to do a study of how jets taking off and landing effects that air molecule," Valentine says. "I've always said, from the same perch, the same ball off of Mike's bat, went into the camera booth. And that was on September 21st. And there were no planes. How fucked up is that?"

The euphoric 3–2 victory over the Braves lifted the Mets two games over .500 for the first time all season. They won again the next day to pull within 3 ½ games of first place, but Armando Benitez blew saves on September 23 and again against the Braves six days later as the last-ditch pennant push fell short.

But baseball was not yet done providing a diversion to New Yorkers in 2001. While the Yankees won the AL East by 13 ½ games, they entered the playoffs as decided underdogs for the first time in the dynasty era. The Seattle Mariners, fueled by Japanese rookie sensation Ichiro Suzuki, won a record 116 regular-season games. The wild card team, the Oakland Athletics, won 102 games—seven more than the Yankees.

Despite having a worse record, the Yankees had home field advantage in the AL Division Series by virtue of winning their division. But the Athletics put the Yankees' dynasty in its greatest jeopardy by winning the first two games in New York. The season, and the era, was in the hands of Mike Mussina, who was opposing Barry Zito, one of the Athletics' trio of young star starting pitchers.

Zito carried a no-hitter into the fifth, when Jorge Posada homered with one out. Mussina limited the Athletics to two hits through 6 ⅔ innings before Jeremy Giambi singled. Terrence Long—acquired by the Athletics from the Mets in the deal that sent Kenny Rogers to Queens in 1999—followed with a double down the first base line.

Shane Spencer retrieved the ball and fired toward the infield as Giambi was waved home. Spencer's throw sailed over the heads of both cutoff men—second baseman Alfonso Soriano and first baseman Tino Martinez.

But Derek Jeter was about to produce a play that would dwarf his defining moments from the 2000 World Series.

Jeter, running toward the right side of the diamond as the play unfolded, followed the path of the ball as it skittered into no-man's-land up the first base line. He sped up, corralled the ball with his bare hand, and backhanded a throw to the plate to catcher Jorge Posada. Giambi didn't slide, and Posada applied the tag to Giambi's leg a split-second before it hit home plate.

The Yankees hung on for the 1–0 victory and won Games Four and Five to remain alive.

"The one thing that we know about Jeter, and why he is who he is: He makes big plays at big times," Yankees third baseman Scott Brosius says.

The Yankees had an easier time in the AL Championship Series rematch with the Mariners, whose magical season sputtered out with a five-game loss. The only team standing between the Yankees and a four-peat—a feat accomplished only by the 1936–39 and 1949–53 Yankees—was a franchise that hadn't even played a game yet when the dynasty began in 1996.

The Arizona Diamondbacks, a 1998 expansion team, reached the World Series in their fourth season thanks to a spate of veteran free agent signings and acquisitions, most notably the 1-2 pitching punch of Randy Johnson and Curt Schilling. The Diamondbacks' first manager was Buck Showalter, who took the job with the fledgling franchise after not being retained by the Yankees following the 1995 season. But Showalter was fired after the 2000 season and replaced by Bob Brenly, who interviewed for the job just before broadcasting the 2000 World Series for FOX.

Before the World Series began, the Diamondbacks followed the lead of Brenly and Schilling, each of whom insisted they were not cowed by facing the Yankees and the supposed magic that enveloped the home team at Yankee Stadium. During the workout day prior to Game One in Arizona, the famously loose-lipped Schilling declared, ". . . mystique and aura, those are dancers in a nightclub. Those are not things we concern ourselves [with] on the ball field."

"We tried to downplay that whole aura and mystique thing, to the point that Curt took it to the next level," Brenly says. "I remember saying to the assembled media that I felt it was patently unfair to the players on the team to say that there's some kind of magic. It's not magic, it's going out and executing and playing good baseball."

The Diamondbacks did just that in winning the first two games in Arizona by a combined margin of 13–1. But the return to New York October 30 would yield one of the most memorable sequences of games ever played.

Before Game Three, President George W. Bush threw out the first pitch. He was the sixth sitting president to throw out the first pitch at a World Series game, but none of his predecessors did so mere weeks after America had been attacked and thrust into war. Bush was fitted with a bulletproof vest before heading to the mound, and one of the "umpires" standing on the field was actually a Secret Service officer.

It was, by any standard, the most somber and serious first pitch in history. But Jeter continued his knack for being in the right place at the right time by providing some levity when he saw Bush warming up in one of the Yankees' batting cages.

"He says, 'Hey, are you gonna throw in front of the mound?'" Bush told ESPN in a *30 for 30* documentary about his first pitch. "I said, 'What do you think?' He said, 'This is Yankee Stadium, you better throw on top of the mound. Otherwise, they'll boo you.' And I said, 'OK, yeah, I'll do that.'

"And just as he's leaving, he turns around and says, 'But don't bounce it, they'll boo you.'"

Bush, wearing an FDNY jacket over his bulletproof vest, indeed stepped atop the mound, waved to the sellout crowd of 55,820, and fired a strike.

Roger Clemens authored another strong postseason start as he out-dueled Brian Anderson to lead the Yankees to a 2–1 victory. The win ensured the World Series would extend into November for the first time ever. Schilling, the Game One starter, started on three days rest in Game Four Halloween night and tossed seven innings of one-run ball.

The Diamondbacks carried a 3–1 lead into the ninth inning and were one out away from taking a three-games-to-one lead when Tino Martinez hit what at the moment stood as the most dramatic homer of the dynasty, a game-tying two-run shot off Byung-Hyun Kim just beyond the wall in right-center field.

Two innings later, Jeter topped Martinez. The clock struck midnight during a nine-pitch duel with Kim that ended at 12:04 a.m., when Jeter hit the game-winning solo homer down the right-field line.

"A game-wining, walk-off homer by Derek Jeter!" bellowed Yankees radio play-by-play man Michael Kay. "He is Mr. November!"

The Diamondbacks displayed impressive resiliency in Game Five, when they carried a 2–0 lead into the ninth inning. Once again, Kim moved within one out of closing out a victory that would put the Diamondbacks one win away from clinching the World Series.

And once again, he gave up a game-tying two-run homer—this one to Scott Brosius, who homered to left field, where Danny Bautista frantically climbed the wall in a futile attempt to catch the ball, just as Steve Finley had done in center field the night before.

"I have never seen anything like it," Tim McCarver said after more than a minute of silence in the booth.

"It borders on the surreal here in the Bronx," Joe Buck added about 15 seconds later.

Alfonso Soriano delivered the game-winning RBI single in the 12th inning to send the Yankees back to Arizona needing only one victory to win a fourth straight title.

But the Diamondbacks, behind Johnson, cruised to a 15–2 win in Game Six to set up a delicious Game Seven—Schilling vs. Clemens. Bautista gave the Diamondbacks the lead with an RBI double in the sixth before the Yankees responded with Tino Martinez's run-scoring single in the top of the seventh.

An inning later Soriano homered off Schilling. Johnson got the final out of the eighth, but with Mariano Rivera entering, it seemed to be too little, too late for Brenly and the Diamondbacks. After working around a single in the eighth, Rivera and the Yankees took the field in the bottom of the ninth three outs away from extending the dynasty.

It all fell apart in 14 frantic pitches. Mark Grace led off with a single. Damian Miller followed with a bunt back to the mound. Rivera, who committed just six errors in 374 regular-season chances over his 19-season career, fired the ball past second base into center field.

Torre visited the mound and implored Rivera and the rest of the infield to just focus on getting one out, especially with Jay Bell—pinch-hitting for Johnson—likely to bunt. Bell did indeed lay down a bunt. Rivera fielded and fired to third for the force, after which Brosius ran the ball back toward the mound instead of firing to first to try and double up the slow-footed Bell. Later, Torre would wonder if his advice impacted the instincts of Brosius, a Gold Glove-winning third baseman.

"Did I put it in Scott's head not to try for a double play? Did I make too much out of being careful?" Torre told ESPN.com's Bob Klapisch in 2004. "I never got a chance to ask him that, because everyone left the clubhouse pretty fast after the game. But I do think about it."

The unraveling continued. Tony Womack followed with a game-tying RBI double to hand Rivera just his second blown save in 26 postseason opportunities. The normally precise Rivera then plunked Craig Counsell—only the second time he'd hit a batter in 298 postseason plate appearances.

Luis Gonzalez, fresh off a season in which he'd hit a franchise-record 57 home runs, stepped to the plate. With the count 0–1, Gonzalez choked up on the bat, something usually done by an unimposing contact hitter just hoping to put the ball in play.

But that's exactly what Gonzalez was trying to do against Rivera's patented cutter. Gonzalez swung and broke his bat on a blooper. It kept carrying right over the drawn-in infield and landed in shallow center field as Bell raced home with the World Series-winning run.

The stunned Yankees walked off the field as a deafening roar filled Bank One Ballpark and the Diamondbacks poured onto the field for a raucous celebration. All the Diamondbacks had to do to become the fastest expansion team to win a championship in baseball history was knock off one of its greatest dynasties.

"It's funny, because leading up to and during the series, we tried to downplay the Yankee dynasty, mystique/aura thing," Brenly says. "But once it was over, it was a point of pride, you know? This is one of the greatest teams in the history of baseball. They were on one of the greatest runs in the history of baseball. And we stopped them. So yeah, we were very proud of that.

"But it was funny how my attitude changed. 'Ahh, they're just another team.' Once we won, they're the greatest team ever!"

The dynasty might have ended even with a Game Seven victory. Paul O'Neill, the beloved warrior, had already announced his plans to retire and was serenaded with chants of "PAUL O'NEILL!" as he stood in right field at Yankee Stadium during the late innings of Game Five. Despite being only 35 years old, Brosius was also planning to retire in order to spend more time with his family.

Tino Martinez was headed for free agency, and George Steinbrenner had his sights set on Jason Giambi, the MVP-winning first baseman of the Oakland Athletics. Chuck Knoblauch, who could no longer play second base due to his throwing issues but was no longer an everyday-caliber offensive player anywhere else on the diamond, was also going to hit the open market.

But it would have been easier for the Yankees to accept the dynasty ending on their terms. Even with the multiple World Series rings on their fingers, players wondered about the ones in 1997 and 2001 that got away.

"You lose in Cleveland the way we did and it's just like you're in shock, you're just numb," O'Neill says. "Now you have to go back to spring training, go through a whole season just to get back to that point again. And I think we realized how quick it can happen."

"For me, 2001 is kind of crushing," Brosius says. "Three in a row and four out of five and being in a fourth straight World Series, you realize how special it was. But especially on the heels of 2001, and 9/11, and the things that happened, the games in New York, the comeback wins out there—to lose that series the way we did it, it still hurts, actually, to this day. When you go back to that Game Seven, it still does hurt."

Even though they didn't four-peat, the enormity of what the Yankees accomplished from 1998 through 2000 has only been magnified over the last two decades, a span in which no team has repeated as World Series champion. Only the Boston Red Sox and San Francisco Giants have won as many as three championships since the end of the Yankees' dynasty (through 2019).

Joe Maddon, who directed the Chicago Cubs to the franchise's first championship in 108 years in 2016, says the rise of analytics has made it more difficult for teams to replicate their success.

"I think everybody's chasing the same players these days," Maddon says. "It's kind of void of the methodologies per team, where the Yankees had a way, the Mets had a way, the Cubs had a way, the [Tampa Bay] Rays had a way. Everybody has the same way right now. So I think on an annual basis, it's hard to really separate yourself because everybody's coming at you from the same sheet of music."

But Maddon also understands, as does Torre, how hard it is for teams to maintain that edge after they've won.

"They had this unique group," Maddon says. "To have a group together like that, that stayed hungry as consistently as they did, is also unusual."

"It's not only our sport, but other sports—we make so much of needing to win this or needing to win that that sometimes when you win it, you sort of say, 'I did it,'" Torre says. "As I say about our players, once you stop to admire what you accomplished, you stop doing it."

***

Four years of increasingly intense regular-season meetings yielded the World Series New Yorkers had waited to see for almost two generations. Without an immediate sequel in 2001, it stood to reason that subsequent installments in the Yankees-Mets rivalry would be less heated.

But first, there was at least one more coda to be written to the most contentious chapter in the history of the modern Subway Series.

Roger Clemens had to bat at Shea Stadium.

Torre was able to shuffle his rotation to ensure Clemens avoided pitching against the Mets at Shea Stadium in 2001. But as much as Torre could protest that he didn't want to feed what he believed to be a media machine steeped in bloodlust, he also knew the only way to try and bring an end to a two-year story was to have Clemens actually oppose the Mets on the road.

"I think it's been blown out of proportion," Torre said prior to the series opener June 14, 2002. "I've been a wimp for not pitching him here last year, or people said he begged off of it. I'd just as soon get it over with."

Of course, in classic Clemens fashion, he managed to get into a beanball controversy in the start prior to his showdown against the Mets. While facing the San Francisco Giants on June 9, Clemens plunked freshly minted single-season home run king Barry Bonds on the right wrist with a 95-mph fastball.

The concept of Bonds, hovering over the plate and wearing enough armor to protect a small country, getting hit wouldn't normally be controversial. But a few days before his start, Clemens promised to pitch inside and declared he would ". . . get that piece of plastic off him."

For Clemens's many critics, watching him hit Bonds in an American League park was a reminder he'd fashioned a reputation as the modern Bob Gibson or Don Drysdale without doing what Gibson and Drysdale did—step into a batter's box three times a game.

"In the National League, he might not be known as 'The Rocket,'"

Giants manager Dusty Baker told reporters afterward. "He may be known as 'Roger the Dodger.'"

Clemens avoided punishment following a visit with Major League Baseball Vice President of On-field Operations Bob Watson, a former Yankees general manager. But would he finally pay a price against the Mets?

The weekend series didn't get off to an encouraging start for the Mets, who dropped the Friday night opener, 4–2, when Robin Ventura—traded to the Yankees the previous December in a rare intracity deal between the rivals—hit a two-run homer in the 10th inning.

The task of trying to even the series—and the score—fell on the shoulders of one of the four starting pitchers who wasn't even a member of the Mets in 2000. Shawn Estes spent the first seven seasons of his career with the San Francisco Giants before being acquired by the Mets nine days after Ventura was sent across town. His teammates spoke of understanding the awkwardness of his predicament: how do you exact revenge for something that happened when you weren't there?

And yet . . .

"But on the other hand, he has to live here for the next six months," team captain John Franco told *Newsday*. "I don't know what he's going to do."

Estes warmed up to the strains of the Jimmy Eat World hit song "The Middle," a self-aware nod to his spot in a surreal situation. With a crowd of 54,347 booing him, Clemens stepped to the plate in the third inning of a scoreless game.

And with his first pitch, Estes . . . threw behind Clemens's rear end, the pitch sailing past Piazza's outstretched glove. Clemens smirked and tapped his helmet towards Estes. Home plate umpire Wally Bell dutifully made the warning motion toward both benches. Mets manager Bobby Valentine took off his hat and ran his hands through his hair.

"I missed my spot," Estes said afterward. "I didn't execute my pitch. You can draw your own conclusions."

"I never doubted Shawn as being a good teammate," Piazza said following the game.

Estes ended up getting fined $750 by Watson for the pitch, which Watson said was a violation of rule 8.02(d) stating a pitcher shall not intentionally throw a pitch at an opponent.

Fortunately for the Mets, they'd get some priceless payback in the coming innings. In the bottom of the third, the Mets took the lead when Rey Ordonez, who led off with a double, raced home after Clemens didn't cover the plate on Estes's bunt up the third base line.

The Mets still led 1–0 in the fifth, when Estes stunned everyone—most notably himself—by hitting a two-run homer off Clemens.

"The home run was not in my dreams," Estes said.

Clemens doubled leading off the sixth but didn't try to score on either Alfonso Soriano's single or Derek Jeter's fly ball. Imagine if he had, and if he'd tried to jar the ball loose from Piazza.

"I'd hate to see where that would have gone," Torre said.

Piazza got the Mets' last laugh in the bottom of the inning, when he hit a leadoff homer—his fourth and final homer off his nemesis. Two outs later, Clemens departed due to a sore foot he said he'd suffered while running the bases.

The Mets went on to win, 8–0. Most everyone was satisfied with the resolution of the Piazza-Clemens feud, with the vocal exception of ESPN analyst Rob Dibble, a noted headhunter in his day who said Estes was a "clown" for missing Clemens.

Estes shrugged off any critics while offering a bit of perspective gleaned from the understanding the world had changed a lot in the two years since Clemens and Piazza became the greatest soap opera in sports.

"With all the tragedy that's happened in the last year, with September 11, I'd say that there's other issues that are involved," Estes said. "I don't see how people can think that way. I just don't understand how someone can want someone to be hurt that bad. I know, regardless of the situation, I wasn't going to make everybody happy."

With interleague play having long ago become a staple of the baseball schedule, and the Yankees and Mets having already played each other in the biggest baseball games possible and Clemens finally having appeared at Shea Stadium, a certain sense of normalcy began to accompany Yankees-Mets games.

"The World Series, there's nothing like it," Mariano Rivera says. "We played the Mets so much it [was] like it was a regular schedule for us. We know that when the season starts, we're going to play the Mets two times. So to me, it wasn't anything different."

Following the 2001 season, the teams also returned to the standards they'd set in the decades before interleague play. The Yankees made the eighth of 13 straight playoffs appearances in 2002, when the Mets fell into last place in the NL East. The Mets finished last again in 2003, when the Yankees won all six games against the Mets—the first season sweep in Subway Series history.

The random and quirky things that transpired during the Subway Series—such as the Mets' Roger Cedeno stealing home against Ted Lilly on June 29, 2002, and the Mets, on their way to another 90-loss season in 2004, enjoying their first three-game sweep of the Yankees—were recognized as part of the cadence of a season, not events magnified by the setting in which they took place.

The retirements of O'Neill and Brosius began the inevitable changing of the guard on the Subway Series stage. Bobby Valentine was fired following the 2002 season. Steve Phillips was fired in June 2003. Clemens "retired" in 2003, the season in which he won his 300th game. Al Leiter expected to finish his career with his favorite childhood team, but he and the Mets couldn't agree on a one-year deal following the 2004 season, and he signed with the Florida Marlins. (Leiter struggled to a 6.64 ERA before being released by the Marlins and finishing the season, and his career, with his original big-league team, the Yankees.)

With the Subway Series back-burnered, the Yankees returned to a more natural rivalry—their decades-long battle for the northeast corridor with the Boston Red Sox. The Yankees were four outs away from being eliminated by the Red Sox in Game Seven of the 2003 AL Championship Series before mounting a stunning rally that ended with Aaron Boone's walk-off 11th-inning homer.

The next season, the Yankees learned what could happen when a fierce, evenly matched rival was allowed to get back into a best-of-seven series and experienced a worst-case scenario even bleaker than losing the 2000 World Series to the Mets.

The Yankees raced out to a three-games-to-none ALCS lead over the Red Sox, whom New York had crushed 19–8 in Game Three. But the Red Sox earned walk-off, extra-inning wins in Games Four and Five—Rivera blew saves in both games—and completed the greatest comeback in baseball history by never trailing in their Games Six and Seven wins in Yankee Stadium. It was only the third time a team in one of the four major North American sports came back from a three-games-to-none deficit to win a best-of seven series. The Red Sox went on to sweep the St. Louis Cardinals to win the World Series for the first time since 1918.

Had this happened to the Yankees four years earlier, jobs almost certainly would have been lost. But George Steinbrenner was less visible following a fainting spell at the funeral for football Hall of Famer Otto Graham in 2003. Rumors of declining health spread and were not quelled by his more vulnerable appearance when he was seen in public.

Steinbrenner spent most of his first three decades as owner trying to get the Yankees a new stadium, one he occasionally threatened to build in New Jersey. But at a press conference in 2006 breaking ground for the new Yankee Stadium across the street from the hallowed "House That Ruth Built," Steinbrenner spoke in a halting voice and for just 25 seconds.

"Enjoy the stadium," Steinbrenner said. "I hope it's wonderful."

The Mets also broke ground on a new stadium in 2006, the same season in which their rebuilding program bore fruit. Hopes for a Subway Series sequel built as the Yankees and Mets both finished with the best records in their respective leagues for the first time.

A second Subway Series would have featured an almost entirely new cast of characters. Steve Phillips's last transaction as general manager was promoting 20-year-old shortstop Jose Reyes to the majors. Alex Rodriguez, whose demands following the 2000 season never gave him a chance to sign with the Mets, was traded to the Yankees in February 2004 following three unhappy seasons with the Texas Rangers.

David Wright, drafted by the Mets with the compensatory pick they received when Mike Hampton signed with the Colorado Rockies following the 2000 season, made his big-league debut in July 2004. Robinson Cano, a then-rare homegrown star for the Yankees, reached the majors in 2005, the same season the Mets began reversing their fortunes with a pair of big-name free agents—center fielder Carlos Beltran and pitcher Pedro Martinez, who became franchise centerpieces as Piazza completed his seven-year contract before spending a season apiece with the San Diego Padres and Oakland Athletics.

Two newcomers to the Subway Series created one of the most entertaining moments in rivalry history May 21, 2005. Mets pitcher Dae-Sung Koo, in the midst of his only big-league season, relieved Kris Benson in the seventh inning and was sent to bat for himself in the bottom of the inning even though Koo had batted just once in the majors—five days earlier, when he didn't move in the batter's box as he looked at three straight called strikes from Cincinnati Reds right-hander Todd Coffey.

Now Koo was going to step to the plate against a left-hander—and not just any left-hander, but the most feared pitcher of his generation: Randy Johnson. Yet on a 1–1 count, Koo swung and laced a double to the warning track in right-center field.

The next batter, Reyes, dropped a sacrifice bunt in front of the plate. Jorge Posada fielded it and fired to first, where second baseman Cano was covering. The throw was a bit wide of the bag, and Cano remained crouched after snaring the ball for the out. Posada continued jogging toward first.

Koo, seeing all of this, raced home from third. Cano, waiting for

Posada to begin heading back toward the plate, double-clutched before throwing as Posada ran backward. Posada caught the ball in between the mound and first base and sprinted to the plate, where he dived and appeared to tag a sliding Koo. But home plate umpire Chuck Meriweather called Koo safe.

In 2006, the Mets and Yankees whetted appetites for a Subway Series sequel when they split six regular-season games, four of which were decided by two runs or fewer. But hopes of another Yankees-Mets World Series perished when the Yankees were knocked out of the AL Division Series in four games by the Detroit Tigers. Rodriguez, hitting just .116 in 43 postseason at-bats since Game Three of the 2004 ALCS, was dropped to the eighth spot in the order for the fourth game.

The elimination of the Yankees left the Mets as the clear favorite to win the World Series. But the 97-win Mets were stunned in the NLCS by the 83-win St. Louis Cardinals, who won Game Seven at Shea Stadium when Beltran, at the plate as the potential NLCS-winning run, struck out looking at a curveball thrown by Cardinals rookie closer Adam Wainwright.

The 2007 chase for a Subway Series featured a familiar face. Roger Clemens's "retirement" following the 2003 season lasted all of 79 days before he signed with his hometown Houston Astros, who had just inked his friend and former Yankees teammate, Andy Pettitte, to a three-year deal as a free agent.

And remarkably, Clemens's return would mean the reopening of his book with Mike Piazza. Clemens not only returned to the diamond in 2004, he won his seventh Cy Young by going 18–4 with a 2.98 ERA in 33 starts. With the All-Star Game being held at Houston's Minute Maid Park, Clemens was the obvious choice to serve as the National League's starting pitcher. The rest of the lineup was selected by a fan vote, which meant for the eighth time in 10 years, the starting catcher would be . . . Mike Piazza.

Both men seemed to enjoy their reunion as much as they would a tax audit.

"I don't have to pitch at him, I'm pitching with him now—we're on the same team," Clemens said before the All-Star Game. "It's not a story that's what's going on here."

"I'm excited for the opportunity," Piazza said, while, according to ESPN.com, rolling his eyes.

Some eyebrows were raised during the first inning of the All-Star Game, when Clemens gave up six runs, three earned. Clemens's fastball was clocked at a mere 91 mph. Was he simply having a bad day? Was he once again struggling in a big-pressure environment? Or was Piazza getting his revenge on Clemens?

"Yeah, Mike told us what was coming," American League manager Joe Torre told the *Washington Post* jokingly (probably).

After three seasons (and two more flirtations with retirement) with the Astros, Clemens returned to the Big Apple on May 7, 2007, when he showed up in Steinbrenner's luxury box at Yankee Stadium and spoke to fans during the seventh-inning stretch.

"Well, they came and got me out of Texas," Clemens said in his familiar drawl.

All it took this time was a prorated contract worth $28 million. Clemens's second start in his second stint with the Yankees was against the Mets at Yankee Stadium. He was surrounded by familiar faces—Bernie Williams played his final game a season earlier, but Rivera, Posada, Jeter, and Pettitte, who returned to the team after the 2006 season, were all still in the Bronx—and the feeling a postseason Subway Series was possible.

But while the Yankees made the playoffs as the AL wild card team, the Mets blew a seven-game NL East lead with 17 games to play. The Mets entered the season finale with a chance to at least force a one-game playoff for the division title or wild card berth, but they missed the postseason entirely when Tom Glavine, who joined Clemens in the 300-win club in August, gave up seven runs while recording just one out in an 8–1 loss to the Florida Marlins.

Two more eras ended when the Yankees were eliminated by the

Cleveland Indians in the AL Division Series, a defeat that finally marked the end of Clemens's career. Torre could not agree to terms on a new contract with the Yankees, bringing an abrupt halt to the most successful managerial stint in New York since Casey Stengel.

Clemens's retirement linked him one more time with his old foe. Piazza also retired following the 2007 season, which made both men eligible for the Hall of Fame in 2013. But no one would have to worry about the awkwardness of the two men sharing an induction stage.

In December 2007, the Mitchell Report—the 20-month investigation into baseball's steroid era overseen by former Senator George Mitchell—was released. Clemens's name was cited 82 times. His former strength coach, Brian McNamee, told Mitchell he injected Clemens with steroids throughout the 1998, 2000, and 2001 seasons.

Clemens sued McNamee for defamation in January 2008 and testified before Congress a month later that he never took performance-enhancing drugs. In 2010, a federal grand jury indicted Clemens on six charges related to his testimony—one count of obstruction, two counts of perjury, and three counts of making false statements.

Clemens was found not guilty in 2012, but the damage to his candidacy was done. In January 2013, he debuted on the ballot and received just 37.6 percent of the vote, well short of the 75 percent necessary for induction. In 2019, the seventh of the maximum 10 years he can remain on the ballot, Clemens received 59.5 percent of the vote.

The Yankees and Mets each played their final seasons in their iconic homes in 2008, but there would be no storybook Subway Series to close the stadia in style. The Yankees, managed by former catcher Joe Girardi, missed the playoffs for the first time since the strike-shortened 1994 season, while the Mets once again squandered a September lead—they were 3 ½ games up in the NL East with 17 to play—and were eliminated from contention with a season-ending 4–2 loss to the Marlins at Shea Stadium.

The Yankees' response to sitting home in October? With George Steinbrenner in declining health, Brian Cashman signed three free agents prior to the 2009 season—pitchers CC Sabathia and A.J. Burnett and first baseman Mark Teixeira—to contracts worth a combined $423.5 million. Fueled by the newcomers, and contributions from the "Core Four" of Rivera, Jeter, Posada, and Pettitte, the Yankees won 103 regular-season games before earning their first World Series since 2000 by beating the Philadelphia Phillies in six games.

The championship season was highlighted by the most memorable and contentious Subway Series games since 2000. On June 12, the visiting Mets were one out away from beating the Yankees in the series opener when Luis Castillo dropped a routine pop-up by Alex Rodriguez as Derek Jeter scored the tying run from second base and Teixeira scored the winning run all the way from first base to give the Yankees a wild 9–8 win.

Afterward, Yankees reliever Brian Bruney said he was particularly happy with the win because it came at the expense of Mets closer Francisco Rodriguez, whose postsave celebrations annoyed Bruney.

"It couldn't happen to a better guy on the mound, either," Bruney said afterward. "He's got a tired act."

Two days later, Rodriguez began shouting at Bruney during batting practice and had to be separated from going after him by players from both teams. On June 28, as the Yankees completed a three-game sweep at Shea Stadium, Rivera earned the 500th save of his career—and collected the first RBI of his career via a bases-loaded walk—in the Yankees' 4–2 victory.

There would be no rematch in October for the Yankees and Mets, the latter of whom were entering an unusual period of austerity.

In December 2008, with "The Great Recession" well underway, Bernard Madoff was arrested for securities fraud. Madoff, who operated his own investment securities firm since 1960, eventually pleaded guilty to overseeing a Ponzi scheme in which $50 billion was lost—including $500 million invested by the Wilpons, the family that owned the Mets.

Between 2009 and 2014, a span in which the Mets endured six straight losing seasons, the team's payroll was cut almost in half—from about $149 million to $85 million. Though Madoff said the Wilpons knew nothing about the Ponzi scheme, the family was among those sued by Irving Picard, the trustee of the Madoff trust. In 2012, the Wilpons reached an agreement to pay $162 million to settle the suit.

The Yankees began a less controversial but no less seismic transformation, as well. After several years of ill health, George Steinbrenner died of a heart attack on July 13, 2010. While the team remained within his family—sons Hal and Hank took over as cochairmen—Steinbrenner's children run the Yankees in a much quieter and fiscally conservative fashion than their dad.

Posada retired following the 2011 season. Rivera planned to do so after 2012 but changed his plans after he suffered a torn ACL while shagging fly balls before a May game against the Kansas City Royals. The seemingly impenetrable Jeter suffered a broken ankle during the 2012 AL Championship Series and missed most of Rivera's final season in 2013.

Rivera was honored by the Mets prior to his last game at Citi Field on May 28, 2013, when the Mets strung together three straight hits in the ninth off Rivera to earn a 2–1 win. It was the first time Rivera blew a save opportunity without recording an out. The Mets earned their first sweep of a regular-season Subway Series, which in 2013 consisted of just four games—back-to-back two-game sets in each stadium.

The Yankees missed the playoffs in both 2013 and 2014—their first back-to-back misses since a franchise-record 13-year drought from 1982 to 1994. Alex Rodriguez was suspended for the entire 2014 season for repeated violations of baseball's performance-enhancing drugs policies.

Rodriguez missed Jeter's farewell tour in 2014. Jeter's final game at Citi Field overshadowed the big-league debut of little-known Mets pitcher Jacob deGrom, who took the loss after allowing one run over seven innings.

Torre, who managed three seasons with the Los Angeles Dodgers before retiring following the 2010 season, was elected to the Hall of

Fame in 2014. His enshrinement made him look prescient: back in 1982, when Torre was managing his first season with the Atlanta Braves following his firing by the Mets, he told *Newsday*'s Marty Noble that he didn't want to win with the Braves any more than he did in New York.

"I want to win wherever I am," Torre said. "The difference is winning in New York is, once you've won, everyone everywhere knows you."

After leaving the dugout, Torre became Major League Baseball's executive vice president of baseball operations, a title modified in 2014 to chief baseball officer. Thanks to his last-chance success with the Yankees, he has become perhaps the most recognizable authority figure in the game.

"Well, I wore a Yankee hat into the Hall of Fame," Torre says. "Had my best years as a player with the Cardinals and started with the Braves. Not that I ignored them, but really, what got me where I was was the opportunity to manage in New York and having the team I had."

Both New York teams returned to the playoffs in 2015. But while the hopes of a Subway Series disappeared when the Yankees lost to the Houston Astros in the AL wild card game, the Mets, led by deGrom and several other 20-something-year-old pitchers, made it all the way to the World Series before falling to the Royals in five games.

The Mets made the playoffs again as a wild card team in 2016, when Piazza, who said he never used PEDs but heard plenty of whispers wondering how he climbed from anonymity to the top of his profession, got into the Hall of Fame on his fourth try.

Piazza was enshrined on July 24—just before the Yankees, on their way to missing the playoffs for just the fourth time in 22 seasons, began rebuilding by trading veteran stars such as Carlos Beltran, Aroldis Chapman, and Andrew Miller and phasing out Rodriguez, who played his final game August 12.

The trade deadline arrived August 1, hours before a Mets-Yankees game at Citi Field.

"That was a helluva run," Yankees general manager Brian Cashman said. “But that run of contention and being legitimately considered a team that could win a championship on a year-in and year-out basis had gone on for a long time. From my perspective there’s no shame in anything that we’ve tried to address today.”

But the Yankees returned to prominence faster than even Cashman could have anticipated. Fueled by the young players drafted, signed, and acquired by Cashman—including outfielder Aaron Judge, who hit a rookie-record 52 homers—the Yankees reached the AL Championship Series in 2017 and fell in seven games to the eventual World Series champion Houston Astros.

In September 2017, Jeter, whose relationship with the Yankees turned frosty after contentious contract negotiations with Cashman in 2010, was part of a group that bought the Miami Marlins. Jeter, whose ownership stake was 4 percent, was named team CEO and promptly made a series of unpopular firings while overseeing a teardown of a once-promising team. The fire sale included the trade of superstar outfielder Giancarlo Stanton—whose $325-million contract runs through 2027—to the Yankees.

Under new manager Aaron Boone in 2018, Stanton and the Yankees earned the wild card with 100 wins before falling in the AL Division Series to the Boston Red Sox, who would also win the World Series.

In 2019, the Yankees, with six starters younger than 30, won 103 games and the AL East before falling in six games to the Astros in the ALCS. The Yankees were eliminated when Chapman, the closer traded to the Chicago Cubs in July 2016 and re-signed by the Yankees the following winter, gave up a walk-off homer to Jose Altuve. It was another reminder of the impossible task of replacing Rivera, the all-time saves leader who earlier in the year became the first player to ever receive unanimous induction into the Hall of Fame. The homer Rivera gave up to Jay Payton in Game Two of the 2000 World Series was the second and last round-tripper he surrendered in 57 postseason games, a span in which he faced 527 batters.

The Mets failed to build on their back-to-back playoff appearances and were a combined 20 games under .500 between 2017 and 2019. But like the Yankees, the Mets featured a promising core of homegrown players who, combined with their crosstown brethren, created another golden era of baseball talent and yielded another generation of good-natured barroom/water cooler arguments amongst Yankees and Mets fans.

Jacob deGrom won the Cy Young in both 2018 and 2019, a feat never before achieved by a New York pitcher. While neither player won the title, Mets infielder Jeff McNeil and Yankees infielder D.J. LeMahieu each led their leagues in batting average for most of 2019. And Judge's rookie home-run record lasted all of two seasons, broken by Pete Alonso, who hit 53 homers in 2019.

While the teams shared similarly talented players, their best players continued to carry themselves in a way reflective of the franchises and their fan bases. Judge assumed the cool, distant, corporate, championship-or-bust air perfected by Jeter and echoed by their fans—many of whom fumed when their team lost in the ALCS in 2019, thereby ensuring the Yankees would go a full decade without appearing in the World Series for the first time since the 1910s.

Alonso, meanwhile, reflected a no-filter exuberance familiar to Mets fans who understand victories and playoff runs are to be cherished. Citi Field was a den of joy for a few weeks throughout the second half of the 2019 season, when the Mets went 15–1 from July 25 through August 10 to get within a half-game of a wild card spot. Alonso devised his own hashtag—#LFGM, with the F standing for an excitedly profane seven-letter word—and began ripping off teammates' shirts following walk-off wins.

Regular-season meetings between the Yankees and Mets continued to generate sellout crowds and draw a veritable melting pot of baseball fans who symbolized the timeless nature of the Subway Series.

During one game at Citi Field in 2019, one row featured a Yankees fan wearing a Judge jersey sitting next to a Mets fan wearing a Noah Syndergaard jersey. In another row, a fan wearing a pinstriped Tom

Seaver jersey sat in between a Yankees fan wearing a Mickey Mantle pinstriped jersey and another Yankees fan sporting Rivera's jersey. In yet another row, a fan wearing a Mantle jersey sat next to a fan wearing an Alonso jersey.

The expectations and experiences for each team were reflected in the reactions of the crowds.

"I felt like whenever there was an opportunity for the Yankees to get on in Citi Field, like when they got the lead, it would get loud," says outfielder Curtis Granderson, who played for the Yankees from 2011 through 2013 and the Mets from 2014 until 2017. "I felt like the Yankees fans wanted to let it be known that we're here, we're stepping in. And when the Mets did well in Yankee Stadium, there was the ability to be loud, but at the same time, it was still kind of withdrawn, because the Yankees fans were still trying to be louder.

"I feel like the Yankees just really wanted to let you know we're here, where the Mets were more like if we're going to win, we're going to enjoy it."

Of course, even the best regular-season game between the Yankees and Mets is only an appetizer for the real Subway Series—a rare dish New Yorkers have enjoyed just once over the last 60-plus years. For observers and, especially, the participants, those five games over six days remain an indelible part of their memories.

Hall of Fame-caliber players clashed on the biggest stage. Role players turned into legends. Luis Sojo's broken bat was sent to Cooperstown, where it stayed until he picked it up because ". . . I'm not Derek Jeter or Mariano or Paul O'Neill. I'm just a Punch-and-Judy hitter. I've got to get my bat."

And there were enough unforgettable moments—and enough what-if possibilities—to generate discussions for decades to come or until the next Subway Series . . . whichever comes first.

"You can't win on a bigger stage than in New York," Yankees outfielder David Justice says. "And the magnitude of it being the Subway

Series and the excitement that was in the city of New York surrounding that World Series—that made it real exciting."

"The Angels have never played the Dodgers, the Cubs have never played the White Sox," Mets manager Bobby Valentine says with a laugh. "The Yankees and the Mets actually played in a frigging World Series in New York! It's like out of a comic book. It was amazing.

"That week and probably the rest of everyone's life would have been so much different if we won it. But it was still absolutely spectacular. Nothing less than that.

"If you weren't there, you can't understand how spectacular it was."

# BIBLIOGRAPHY


**INTERVIEWS**

Benny Agbayani
Lindsay Berra
Bob Brenly
Scott Brosius
Rick Cerrone
Chris Chambliss
David Cone
Jack Fisher
Todd Frazier
Curtis Granderson
Lenny Harris
Jay Horwitz
Todd Hundley
Ron Hunt
Butch Huskey
David Justice

Jerry Koosman
Skip Lockwood
Joe Maddon
Don Mattingly
Lee Mazzilli
Joe McEwing
Felix Millan
Jeff Nelson
Keith Olbermann
Paul O'Neill
Jay Payton
Steve Phillips
Todd Pratt
Mariano Rivera
Luis Sojo
Darryl Strawberry
Joe Torre
Bobby Valentine
Jose Vizcaino
Turk Wendell
Todd Zeile

## BOOKS

Clemens, Roger and Gammons, Peter. *Rocket Man: The Roger Clemens Story*. New York: The Stephen Greene Press, Inc.,1987.

Donnelly, Chris. *Doc, Donnie, the Kid, And Billy Brawl: How the 1985 Mets And Yankees Fought for New York's Baseball Soul.* Lincoln, Nebraska: University of Nebraska Press, 2019.

Golenbock, Peter. *Bums: An Oral History of the Brooklyn Dodgers*. New York: G.P. Putnam's Sons, 1984.

Kahn, Roger. *The Era 1947–1957: When the Yankees, the Giants, and the Dodgers Ruled the World.* New York: Ticknor & Fields, 1993.

Lyle, Sparky and Golenbock, Peter. *The Bronx Zoo*. New York: Crown Publishers, Inc., 1979.

Pearlman, Jeff. *The Rocket That Fell to Earth: Roger Clemens and the Rage for Baseball Immortality*. New York: HarperCollins Publishers, 2009.

Piazza, Mike and Wheeler, Lonnie. *Long Shot*. New York: Simon & Schuster, 2013.

Topel, Brett. *When Shea Was Home: The Story Of the 1975 Mets, Yankees, Giants, and Jets*. New York: Sports Publishing, 2016.

Torre, Joe and Verducci, Tom. *The Yankee Years*. New York: Doubleday, 2009.

## NEWSPAPERS/PERIODICALS/GUIDES/WEBSITES/ TELEVISION SHOWS

Associated Press

*Bergen Record*

*ESPN The Magazine*

*Hartford Courant*

*Los Angeles Times*

*Mets Magazine*

*Newsday*

*New York Daily News*

*New York Mets Inside Pitch*

New York Mets media guide (many seasons)

*New York Post*

*New York Times*

New York Yankees media guide (many seasons)

*San Francisco Chronicle*

*Sport*

*Sports Illustrated*

*Washington Post*

ASAPSports.com

Baseball-Reference.com
CBSSports.com
ESPN.com
MLB.com
SABR.org
SI.com
SportsOnEarth.com
YouTube.com
*30 For 30*